STP 9-94E12-SM-TG, C1

Change No. 1

Headquarters
Department of the Army
Washington, DC, 15 October 2014

SOLDIER'S MANUAL AND TRAINING GUIDE

MOS 94E

RADIO AND COMMUNICATIONS SECURITY (COMSEC) REPAIRER

SKILL LEVELS 1 AND 2

1. Change 1 to STP 9-94E12-SM-TG, 29 July 2014, corrects Performance Steps and Performance Measures.

2. STP 9-94E12-SM-TG, 29 July 2014 is changed as follows:

Remove Old Pages	Insert New Pages
3-13 – 3-15	3-13 – 3-15
References-1	References-1

3. File this transmittal sheet in front of the publication for reference purposes.

DISTRIBUTION RESTRICTION: Approved for public release; distribution is unlimited.

By order of the Secretary of the Army:

RAYMOND T. ODIERNO
General, United States Army
Chief of Staff

Official:

GERALD B. O'KEEFE
Administrative Assistant to the
Secretary of the Army
1425202

DISTRIBUTION:
Active Army, Army National Guard, and United States Army Reserve: Distributed in electronic media only
(EMO).

PIN: 104465-001

STP 9-94E12-SM-TG

SOLDIER TRAINING
PUBLICATION
No.9-94E12-SM-TG

HEADQUARTERS
DEPARTMENT OF THE ARMY
Washington, DC, 29 July 2014

Soldier's Manual and Training Guide

MOS 94E

RADIO AND COMMUNICATIONS SECURITY (COMSEC) REPAIRER, SKILL LEVELS 1 AND 2

TABLE OF CONTENTS

PREFACE

This publication is for skill levels SL1 and SL2 soldiers holding military occupational specialty (MOS) MOS 94E and for trainers and first-line supervisors. It contains standardized training objectives, in the form of task summaries, to train and evaluate soldiers on critical tasks that support unit missions during wartime. Trainers and first-line supervisors should ensure soldiers holding MOS/SL MOS 94ESL1/SL2 have access to this publication. This STP is available for download from the Reimer Digital Library (RDL).

This publication applies to the Active Army, the Army National Guard (ARNG)/Army National Guard of the United States (ARNGUS), and the U.S. Army Reserve (USAR), unless otherwise stated.

The proponent of this publication is HQ, TRADOC. Send comments and recommendations on DA Form 2028 (Recommended Changes to Publications and Blank Forms) directly to Commander, CASCOM SCOE (ATCL-TDF), G-3 Training & Doctrine Development, SUITE 1036, 2221 Adams Ave, Fort Lee, VA 23801-2102.

This page intentionally left blank.

CHAPTER 1

Introduction

1.1 General

The soldier training publication (STP) identifies the individual military occupational specialty (MOS) training requirements for soldiers in various specialties, for example, another source of STP task data is the Central Army Registry (CAR) at https://www.train.army.mil/. Commanders, trainers, and soldiers should use the STP to plan, conduct, and evaluate individual training in units. The STP is the primary MOS reference to support the self-development and training of every soldier in the unit. It is used with the Soldier's Manual of Common Tasks, collective training products, and ADRP 7-0, Training Units and Developing Leaders, to establish effective training plans and programs that integrate soldier, leader, and collective tasks. This chapter explains how to use the STP in establishing an effective individual training program. It includes doctrinal principles and implications outlined in ADRP 7-0. Based on these guidelines, commanders and unit trainers must tailor the information to meet the requirements for their specific unit.

1.2 Training Requirement

Every soldier, noncommissioned officer (NCO), warrant officer, and officer has one primary mission — to be trained and ready to fight and win our nation's wars. Success in battle does not happen by accident; it is a direct result of tough, realistic, and challenging training.

    a.   Operational Environment.

    (1)   Commanders and leaders at all levels must conduct training with respect to a wide variety of operational missions across the full spectrum of operations. These operations may include combined arms, joint, multinational, and interagency considerations, and span the entire breadth of terrain and environmental possibilities. Commanders must strive to set the daily training conditions as closely as possible to those expected for actual operations.

    (2)   The operational missions of the Army include not only war, but also military operations other than war (MOOTW). Operations may be conducted as major combat operations, a small-scale contingency, or a peacetime military engagement. Offensive and defensive operations normally dominate military operations in war along with some small-scale contingencies. Stability operations and support operations dominate in MOOTW. Commanders at all echelons may combine different types of operations simultaneously and sequentially to accomplish missions in war and MOOTW. These missions require training since future conflict will likely involve a mix of combat and MOOTW, often concurrently. The range of possible missions complicates training. Army forces cannot train for every possible mission; they train for war and prepare for specific missions as time and circumstances permit.

    (3)   One type of MOOTW is the Chemical, Biological, Radiological, Nuclear, and High-Yield Explosive (CBRNE) event. To assist commanders and leaders in training their units, CBERNE-related information is being included in AMEDD mission training plans (MTPs). Even

though most collective tasks within an MTP may support a CBRNE event, the ones that will most directly be impacted are clearly indicated with a statement in the CONDITION that reads: "THIS TASK MAY BE USED TO SUPPORT A CBRNE EVENT." These collective tasks and any supporting individual tasks in this soldier's manual should be considered for training emphasis.

      (4)   Our forces today use a train-alert-deploy sequence. We cannot count on the time or opportunity to correct or make up training deficiencies after deployment. Maintaining forces that are ready now, places increased emphasis on training and the priority of training. This concept is a key link between operational and training doctrine.

      (5)   Units train to be ready for war based on the requirements of a precise and specific mission. In the process they develop a foundation of combat skills that can be refined based on the requirements of the assigned mission. Upon alert, commanders assess and refine from this foundation of skills. In the train-alert-deploy process, commanders use whatever time the alert cycle provides to continue refinement of mission-focused training. Training continues during time available between alert notification and deployment, between deployment and employment, and even during employment as units adapt to the specific battlefield environment and assimilate combat replacements.

    b.   How the Army Trains the Army.

      (1)   Training is a team effort and the entire Army — Department of the Army Commands (ACOMs), the institutional training base, units, the combat training centers (CTCs), each individual soldier, and the civilian workforce — has a role that contributes to force readiness. Department of the Army and ACOMs are responsible for resourcing the Army to train. The Institutional Army, including schools, training centers, and NCO academies, for example, train soldiers and leaders to take their place in units in the Army by teaching the doctrine and tactics, techniques, and procedures (TTP). Units, leaders, and individuals train to standard on their assigned critical individual tasks. The unit trains first as an organic unit and then as an integrated component of a team. Before the unit can be trained to function as a team, each soldier must be trained to perform their individual supporting tasks to standard. Operational deployments and major training opportunities, such as major training exercises, CTCs provide rigorous, realistic, and stressful training and operational experience under actual or simulated combat and operational conditions to enhance unit readiness and produce bold, innovative leaders. The result of this Army-wide team effort is a training and leader development system that is unrivaled in the world. Effective training produces the force — soldiers, leaders, and units — that can successfully execute any assigned mission.

      (2)   The Army Training and Leader Development Model (Figure 1-1) centers on developing trained and ready units led by competent and confident leaders. The model depicts an important dynamic that creates a lifelong learning process. The three core domains that shape the critical learning experiences throughout a soldier's and leader's time span are the operational, institutional, and self-development domains. Together, these domains interact using feedback and assessment from various sources and methods to maximize warfighting readiness. Each domain has specific, measurable actions that must occur to develop our leaders.

* The operational domain includes home station training, CTC rotations, and joint training exercises and deployments that satisfy national objectives. Each of these actions provides foundational experiences for soldier, leader, and unit development.

* The institutional domain focuses on educating and training soldiers and leaders on the key knowledge, skills, and attributes required to operate in any environment. It includes individual, unit and joint schools, and advanced education.

* The self-development domain, both structured and informal, focuses on taking those actions necessary to reduce or eliminate the gap between operational and institutional experiences.

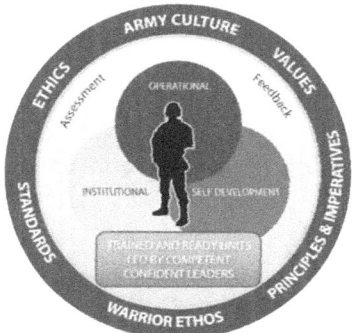

Figure 1-1. Army Training and Leader Development Model

    (3)   Throughout this lifelong learning and experience process, there is formal and informal assessment and feedback of performance to prepare leaders and soldiers for their next level of responsibility. Assessment is the method used to determine the proficiency and potential of leaders against a known standard. Feedback must be clear, formative guidance directly related to the outcome of training events measured against standards.

    c.   Leader Training and Leader Development.

    (1)   Competent and confident leaders are a prerequisite to the successful training of units. It is important to understand that leader training and leader development are integral parts of unit readiness. Leaders are inherently soldiers first and should be technically and tactically proficient in basic soldier skills. They are also adaptive, capable of sensing their environment, adjusting the plan when appropriate, and properly applying the proficiency acquired through training.

    (2)   Leader training is an expansion of these skills that qualifies them to lead other soldiers. As such, doctrine and principles of training require the same level of attention of senior commanders. Leader training occurs in the Institutional Army, the unit, the CTCs, and through self-development. Leader training is just one portion of leader development.

    (3)   Leader development is the deliberate, continuous, sequential, and progressive process, grounded in Army values, that grows soldiers and civilians into competent and confident leaders capable of decisive action. Leader development is achieved through the life-long synthesis of the knowledge, skills, and experiences gained through institutional training and education, organizational training, operational experience, and self-development. Commanders play the key roll in leader development that ideally produces tactically and technically competent, confident, and adaptive leaders who act with boldness and initiative in dynamic, complex situations to execute mission-type orders achieving the commander's intent.

(4)   A life cycle management diagram for soldiers is on page 1-5. You can find more information and check for updates at http://das.cs.amedd.army.mil/ooc.htm (scroll down to LIFE CYCLE MANAGEMENT, select ENLISTED, and find the appropriate tab along the bottom). This information, combined with the MOS Training Plan in Chapter 2, forms the career development model for the MOS.

d.   Training Responsibility. Soldier and leader training and development continue in the unit. Using the institutional foundation, training in organizations and units focuses and hones individual and team skills and knowledge.

(1)   Commander Responsibility.

(a)   The unit commander is responsible for the wartime readiness of all elements in the formation. The commander is, therefore, the primary trainer of the organization and is responsible for ensuring that all training is conducted in accordance with the STP to the Army standard.

(b)   Commanders ensure STP standards are met during all training. If a soldier fails to meet established standards for identified MOS tasks, the soldier must retrain until the tasks are performed to standard. Training to standard on MOS tasks is more important than completion of a unit training event. The objective is to focus on sustaining MOS proficiency — this is the critical factor commanders must adhere to when training individual soldiers in units.

(2)   NCO Responsibility.

(a)   A great strength of the US Army is its professional NCO Corps who takes pride in being responsible for the individual training of soldiers, crews, and small teams. The NCO support channel parallels and complements the chain of command. It is a channel of communication and supervision from the Command Sergeant Major (CSM) to the First Sergeants (1SGs) and then to other NCOs and enlisted personnel. NCOs train soldiers to the non-negotiable standards published in STPs. Commanders delegate authority to NCOs in the support channel as the primary trainers of individual, crew, and small team training. Commanders hold NCOs responsible for conducting standards-based, performance-oriented, battle-focused training and providing feedback on individual, crew, and team proficiency. Commanders define responsibilities and authority of their NCOs to their staffs and subordinates.

(b)   NCOs continue the soldierization process of newly assigned enlisted soldiers, and begin their professional development. NCOs are responsible for conducting standards-based, performance-oriented, battle-focused training. They identify specific individual, crew, and small team tasks that support the unit's collective mission essential tasks; plan, prepare, rehearse, and execute training; and evaluate training and conduct after action reviews (AARs) to provide feedback to the commander on individual, crew, and small team proficiency. Senior NCOs coach junior NCOs to master a wide range of individual tasks.

(3)   Soldier Responsibility. Each soldier is responsible for performing individual tasks identified by the first-line supervisor based on the unit's mission essential task list (METL). Soldiers must perform tasks to the standards included in the task summary. If soldiers have questions about tasks or which tasks in this manual they must perform, they are responsible for asking their first-line supervisor for clarification, assistance, and guidance. First-line supervisors know how to perform each task or can direct soldiers to appropriate training materials, including current field manuals, technical manuals, and Army regulations. Soldiers are responsible for using these materials to maintain performance. They are also responsible for maintaining

standard performance levels of all Soldier's Manual of Common Tasks at their current skill level and below. Periodically, soldiers should ask their supervisor or another soldier to check their performance to ensure that they can perform the tasks.

1.3 Battle-Focused Training

Battle focus is a concept used to derive peacetime training requirements from assigned and anticipated missions. The priority of training in units is to train to standard on the wartime mission. Battle focus guides the planning, preparation, execution, and assessment of each organization's training program to ensure its members train as they are going to fight. Battle focus is critical throughout the entire training process and is used by commanders to allocate resources for training based on wartime and operational mission requirements. Battle focus enables commanders and staffs at all echelons to structure a training program that copes with non-mission-related requirements while focusing on mission essential training activities. It is recognized that a unit cannot attain proficiency to standard on every task whether due to time or other resource constraints. However, unit commanders can achieve a successful training program by consciously focusing on a reduced number of METL tasks that are essential to mission accomplishment.

a.   Linkage between METL and STP. A critical aspect of the battle focus concept is to understand the responsibility for and the linkage between the collective mission essential tasks and the individual tasks that support them. For example, the commander and the CSM/1SG must jointly coordinate the collective mission essential tasks and supporting individual tasks on which the unit will concentrate its efforts during a given period. This task hierarchy is provided in the task database at the Central Army Registry (CAR). The CSM/1SG must select the specific individual tasks that support each collective task to be trained. Although NCOs have the primary role in training and sustaining individual soldier skills, officers at every echelon remain responsible for training to established standards during both individual and collective training. Battle focus is applied to all missions across the full spectrum of operations.

b.   Relationship of STPs to Battle-focused Training. The two key components of any STP are the soldier's manual (SM) and trainer's guide (TG). Each gives leaders important information to help implement the battle-focused training process. The trainer's guide relates soldier and leader tasks in the MOS and skill level to duty positions and equipment. It states where the task is trained, how often training should occur to sustain proficiency, and who in the unit should be trained. As leaders assess and plan training, they should rely on the trainer's guide to help identify training needs.

(1)   Leaders conduct and evaluate training based on Army-wide training objectives and on the task standards published in the soldier's manual task summaries or in the Reimer Digital Library. The task summaries ensure that --

* Trainers in every unit and location define task standards the same way
* Trainers evaluate all soldiers to the same standards

(2)   Table 1-1 shows how battle-focused training relates to the trainer's guide and soldier's manual:

* The left column shows the steps involved in training soldiers.
* The right column shows how the STP supports each of these steps.

Table 1-1. Relationship of Battle-focused Training and STP

BATTLE-FOCUS PROCESS	STP SUPPORT PROCESS
Select supporting soldier tasks	Use TG to relate tasks to METL
Conduct training assessment	Use TG to define what soldier tasks to assess
Determine training objectives	Use TG to set objectives
Determine strategy; plan for training	Use TG to relate soldier tasks to strategy
Conduct pre-execution checks	Use SM task summary as source for task performance
Execute training; conduct after action review	Use SM task summary as source for task performance
Evaluate training against established standards	Use SM task summary as standard for evaluation

1.4 Task Summary Format

Task summaries outline the wartime performance requirements of each critical task in the SM. They provide the soldier and the trainer with the information necessary to prepare, conduct, and evaluate critical task training. As a minimum, task summaries include information the soldier must know and the skills that he must perform to standards for each task. The format of the task summaries included in this SM is as follows:

a. Task Title. The task title identifies the action to be performed.

b. Task Number. A 10-digit number identifies each task or skill. This task number, along with the task title, must be included in any correspondence pertaining to the task.

c. Conditions. The task conditions identify all the equipment, tools, references, job aids, and supporting personnel that the soldier needs to use to perform the task in wartime. This section identifies any environmental conditions that can alter task performance, such as visibility, temperature, or wind. This section also identifies any specific cues or events that trigger task performance, such as a chemical attack or identification of a threat vehicle.

d. Standards. The task standards describe how well and to what level the task must be performed under wartime conditions. Standards are typically described in terms of accuracy, completeness, and speed.

e. Performance Steps. This section includes a detailed outline of information on how to perform the task. Additionally, some task summaries include safety statements and notes. Safety statements (danger, warning, and caution) alert users to the possibility of immediate death, personal injury, or damage to equipment. Notes provide a small, extra supportive explanation or hint relative to the performance steps.

f. Evaluation Preparation (when used). This subsection indicates necessary modifications to task performance in order to train and evaluate a task that cannot be trained to the wartime standard under wartime conditions. It may also include special training and evaluation preparation instructions to accommodate these modifications and any instructions that should be given to the soldier before evaluation.

g.   Performance Measures. This evaluation guide identifies the specific actions that the soldier must do to successfully complete the task. These actions are listed in a GO/NO-GO format for easy evaluation. Each evaluation guide contains an evaluation guidance statement that indicates the requirements for receiving a GO on the evaluation.

h.   References. This section identifies references that provide more detailed and thorough explanations of task performance requirements than those given in the task summary description.

1.5 Training Execution

All good training, regardless of the specific collective, leader, and individual tasks being executed, must comply with certain common requirements. These include adequate preparation, effective presentation and practice, and thorough evaluation. The execution of training includes preparation for training, conduct of training, and recovery from training.

a.   Preparation for Training. Formal near-term planning for training culminates with the publication of the unit training schedule. Informal planning, detailed coordination, and preparation for executing the training continue until the training is performed. Commanders and other trainers use training meetings to assign responsibility for preparation of all scheduled training. Preparation for training includes selecting tasks to be trained, planning the conduct of the training, training the trainers, reconnaissance of the site, issuing the training execution plan, and conducting rehearsals and pre-execution checks. Pre-execution checks are preliminary actions commanders and trainers use to identify responsibility for these and other training support tasks. They are used to monitor preparation activities and to follow up to ensure planned training is conducted to standard. Pre-execution checks are a critical portion of any training meeting. During preparation for training, battalion and company commanders identify and eliminate potential training distracters that develop within their own organizations. They also stress personnel accountability to ensure maximum attendance at training.

(1)   Subordinate leaders, as a result of the bottom-up feed from internal training meetings, identify and select the individual tasks necessary to support the identified training objectives. Commanders develop the tentative plan to include requirements for preparatory training, concurrent training, and training resources. At a minimum, the training plan should include confirmation of training areas and locations, training ammunition allocations, training simulations and simulators availability, transportation requirements, soldier support items, a risk management analysis, assignment of responsibility for the training, designation of trainers responsible for approved training, and final coordination. The time and other necessary resources for retraining must also be an integral part of the original training plan.

(2)   Leaders, trainers, and evaluators are identified, trained to standard, and rehearsed prior to the conduct of the training. Leaders and trainers are coached on how to train, given time to prepare, and rehearsed so that training will be challenging and doctrinally correct. Commanders ensure that trainers and evaluators are not only tactically and technically competent on their training tasks, but also understand how the training relates to the organization's METL. Properly prepared trainers, evaluators, and leaders project confidence and enthusiasm to those being trained. Trainer and leader training is a critical event in the preparation phase of training. These individuals must demonstrate proficiency on the selected tasks prior to the conduct of training.

(3)   Commanders, with their subordinate leaders and trainers, conduct site reconnaissance, identify additional training support requirements, and refine and issue the training execution plan. The training plan should identify all those elements necessary to ensure the conduct of training to standard. Rehearsals are essential to the execution of good training. Realistic, standards-based, performance-oriented training requires rehearsals for trainers, support personnel, and evaluators. Preparing for training in Reserve Component (RC) organizations can require complex pre-execution checks. RC trainers must often conduct detailed coordination to obtain equipment, training support system products, and ammunition from distant locations. In addition, RC pre-execution checks may be required to coordinate Active Component assistance from the numbered CONUSA, training support divisions, and directed training affiliations.

b.   Conduct of Training. Ideally, training is executed using the crawl-walk-run approach. This allows and promotes an objective, standards-based approach to training. Training starts at the basic level. Crawl events are relatively simple to conduct and require minimum support from the unit. After the crawl stage, training becomes incrementally more difficult, requiring more resources from the unit and home station, and increasing the level of realism. At the run stage, the level of difficulty for the training event intensifies. Run stage training requires optimum resources and ideally approaches the level of realism expected in combat. Progression from the walk to the run stage for a particular task may occur during a one-day training exercise or may require a succession of training periods over time. Achievement of the Army standard determines progression between stages.

(1)   In crawl-walk-run training, the tasks and the standards remain the same; however, the conditions under which they are trained change. Commanders may change the conditions, for example, by increasing the difficulty of the conditions under which the task is being performed, increasing the tempo of the task training, increasing the number of tasks being trained, or by increasing the number of personnel involved in the training. Whichever approach is used, it is important that all leaders and soldiers involved understand in which stage they are currently training and understand the Army standard.

(2)   An AAR is immediately conducted and may result in the need for additional training. Any task that was not conducted to standard should be retrained. Retraining should be conducted at the earliest opportunity. Commanders should program time and other resources for retraining as an integral part of their training plan. Training is incomplete until the task is trained to standard. Soldiers will remember the standard enforced, not the one discussed.

c.   Recovery from Training. The recovery process is an extension of training, and once completed, it signifies the end of the training event. At a minimum, recovery includes conduct of maintenance training, turn-in of training support items, and the conduct of AARs that review the overall effectiveness of the training just completed.

(1)   Maintenance training is the conduct of post-operations preventive maintenance checks and services, accountability of organizational and individual equipment, and final inspections. Class IV, Class V, TADSS, and other support items are maintained, accounted for, and turned-in, and training sites and facilities are closed out.

(2)   AARs conducted during recovery focus on collective, leader, and individual task performance, and on the planning, preparation, and conduct of the training just completed. Unit AARs focus on individual and collective task performance, and identify shortcomings and the training required to correct deficiencies. AARs with leaders focus on tactical judgment. These

AARs contribute to leader learning and provide opportunities for leader development. AARs with trainers and evaluators provide additional opportunities for leader development.

1.6 Training Assessment

Assessment is the commander's responsibility. It is the commander's judgment of the organization's ability to accomplish its wartime operational mission. Assessment is a continuous process that includes evaluating individual training, conducting an organizational assessment, and preparing a training assessment. The commander uses his experience, feedback from training evaluations, and other evaluations and reports to arrive at his assessment. Assessment is both the end and the beginning of the training management process. Training assessment is more than just training evaluation, and encompasses a wide variety of inputs. Assessments include such diverse systems as training, force integration, logistics, and personnel, and provide the link between the unit's performance and the Army standard. Evaluation of training is, however, a major component of assessment. Training evaluations provide the commander with feedback on the demonstrated training proficiency of soldiers, leaders, battle staffs, and units. Commanders cannot personally observe all training in their organization and, therefore, gather feedback from their senior staff officers and NCOs.

a. Evaluation of Training. Training evaluations are a critical component of any training assessment. Evaluation measures the demonstrated ability of soldiers, commanders, leaders, battle staffs, and units against the Army standard. Evaluation of training is integral to standards-based training and is the cornerstone of leader training and leader development. STPs describe standards that must be met for each soldier task.

(1) All training must be evaluated to measure performance levels against the established Army standard. The evaluation can be as fundamental as an informal, internal evaluation performed by the leader conducting the training. Evaluation is conducted specifically to enable the individual undergoing the training to know whether the training standard has been achieved. Commanders must establish a climate that encourages candid and accurate feedback for the purpose of developing leaders and trained soldiers.

(2) Evaluation of training is not a test; it is not used to find reasons to punish leaders and soldiers. Evaluation tells soldiers whether or not they achieved the Army standard and, therefore, assists them in determining the overall effectiveness of their training plans. Evaluation produces disciplined soldiers, leaders, and units. Training without evaluation is a waste of time and resources.

(3) Evaluations are used by leaders as an opportunity to coach and mentor soldiers. A key element in developing leaders is immediate, positive feedback that coaches and leads subordinate leaders to achieve the Army standard. This is a tested and proven path to develop competent, confident adaptive leaders.

b. Evaluators. Commanders must plan for formal evaluation and must ensure the evaluators are trained. These evaluators must also be trained as facilitators to conduct AARs that elicit maximum participation from those being trained. External evaluators will be certified in the tasks they are evaluating and normally will not be dual-hatted as a participant in the training being executed.

c. Role of Commanders and Leaders. Commanders ensure that evaluations take place at each echelon in the organization. Commanders use this feedback to teach, coach, and mentor their subordinates. They ensure that every training event is evaluated as part of training execution and that every trainer conducts evaluations. Commanders use evaluations to focus command attention by requiring evaluation of specific mission essential and battle tasks. They also take advantage of evaluation information to develop appropriate lessons learned for distribution throughout their commands.

d. After Action Review. The AAR, whether formal or informal, provides feedback for all training. It is a structured review process that allows participating soldiers, leaders, and units to discover for themselves what happened during the training, why it happened, and how it can be done better. The AAR is a professional discussion that requires the active participation of those being trained.

1.7 Training Support

This manual includes the following information which provides additional training support information.

a. Glossary. The glossary, which follows the last appendix, is a single comprehensive list of acronyms, abbreviations, definitions, and letter symbols.

b. References. This section contains two lists of references, required and related, which support training of all tasks in this SM. Required references are listed in the conditions statement and are required for the Soldier to do the task. Related references are materials that provide more detailed information and a more thorough explanation of task performance.

CHAPTER 2

Training Guide

2.1 General

The MOS Training Plan (MTP) identifies the essential components of a unit training plan for individual training. Units have different training needs and requirements based on differences in environment, location, equipment, dispersion, and similar factors. Therefore, the MTP should be used as a guide for conducting unit training and not a rigid standard. The MTP consists of two parts. Each part is designed to assist the commander in preparing a unit training plan which satisfies integration, cross training, training up, and sustainment training requirements for soldiers in this MOS.

Part One of the MTP shows the relationship of an MOS skill level between duty position and critical tasks. These critical tasks are grouped by task commonality into subject areas.

Section I lists subject area numbers and titles used throughout the MTP. These subject areas are used to define the training requirements for each duty position within an MOS.

Section II identifies the total training requirement for each duty position within an MOS and provides a recommendation for cross training and train-up/merger training.

- **Duty Position Column**. This column lists the duty positions of the MOS, by skill level, which have different training requirements.

- **Subject Area Column**. This column lists, by numerical key (see Section I), the subject areas a soldier must be proficient in to perform in that duty position.

- **Cross Train Column**. This column lists the recommended duty position for which soldiers should be cross trained.

- **Train-up/Merger Column**. This column lists the corresponding duty position for the next higher skill level or MOSC the soldier will merge into on promotion.

Part Two lists, by general subject areas, the critical tasks to be trained in an MOS and the type of training required (resident, integration, or sustainment).

- **Subject Area Column**. This column lists the subject area number and title in the same order as Section I, Part One of the MTP.

- **Task Number Column**. This column lists the task numbers for all tasks included in the subject area.

- **Title Column**. This column lists the task title for each task in the subject area.

- **Training Location Column**. This column identifies the training location and the Leadership Domain (Institutional, Operational, or Self-Development) where the task is first trained to soldier training publications standards. If the task is first trained to standard in the unit, the word "OP" will be in this column. If the task is first trained to standard in the training base, it will identify, by brevity code (S-D, INST), the resident course where the task was taught. Figure 2-1 contains a list of training locations and their corresponding brevity codes.

Table 2-1. Training Locations

Brevity Code	Training Locations
ASI/SD	Additional Skill Identifier/Special Duty
AIT	Advanced Individual Training
ALC	Advanced Leader Course
SLC	Senior Leader Course
INST	Institutional
OP	Operational/Unit

Sustainment Training Frequency Column. This column indicates the recommended frequency at which the tasks should be trained to ensure soldiers maintain task proficiency. Table 2-2 identifies the frequency codes used in this column.

Table 2-2. Sustainment Training Frequency Codes

Code	Meaning
BA	Biannually
AN	Annually
SA	Semi-annually
QT	Quarterly
BM	Bimonthly
MO	Monthly
BW	Biweekly
WK	Weekly
DA	Daily
HR	Hourly

Sustainment Training Skill Level Column. This column lists the skill levels of the MOS for which soldiers must receive sustainment training to ensure they maintain proficiency to soldier's manual standards.

2-2. Part One, Section I. Subject Area Codes.

Skill Level SL1
  1 Receivers-Transmitters
  2 Auxiliary Equipment
  3 Power Supplies
  4 Communications Security (COMSEC)
  5 Security

Skill Level SL2
  6 Maintenance Administration

Table 2-3. Duty Position Training Requirements

2-3. Part One, Section II, Duty Position Training Requirements.				
SKILL LEVEL	DUTY POSITION	SUBJECT AREAS	CROSS TRAIN	TRAIN-UP/MERGER
SL1	RADIO REPAIRER	1-5	N/A	94E1 Radio COMSEC Repairer
SL2	RADIO SUPERVISOR	1-6	N/A	94E2 Radio COMSEC SUPV

2-4. Part Two, Critical Tasks List.

Table 2-4. MOS Training Plan, Critical Tasks List

MOS TRAINING PLAN MOS 94E				
CRITICAL TASKS				
Task Number	Title	Training Location	Sust Tng Freq	Sust Tng SI
Skill Level SL1				
Subject Area 1 Receivers-Transmitters				
091-94E-1021	Repair Receiver-Transmitter RT-1523(*)(C)/U	AIT	OT	1
091-94E-1703	Repair Radio Set AN/PRC-90(*)	UNIT	AN	1
091-94E-1402	Repair Receiver-Transmitter RT-(*)/ARC-164(V)(*)	AIT	OT	1
091-94E-1059	Repair AN/PSC-5(*)	AIT	OT	1
091-94E-1067	Maintain RT-(*)/ARC-231(*)	AIT	OT	1
091-94E-1068	Maintain High Frequency (HF) Radios	AIT	OT	1
091-94E-1302	Repair Receiver-Transmitter RT-(*)/ARC-186(V)(*)	AIT	OT	1
091-94E-1202	Repair Receiver-Transmitter RT-(*)/ARC-201(V)(*)	AIT	OT	1
091-94E-1702	Test the AN/PRC-112(*)	UNIT	AN	1
Subject Area 2 Auxiliary Equipment				
091-94E-1102	Repair Communications System Control C-6533(*)/ARC	AIT	OT	1
091-94E-1006	Repair Control Monitor C-11291(*)/VRC	UNIT	AN	1
091-94E-1007	Repair Remote Control Unit C-11561 (C)/U	UNIT	AN	1
091-94E-1005	Repair Amplifier-Adapter Vehicular AM-7239(*)/VRC	AIT	OT	1
Subject Area 3 Power Supplies				
091-94E-1013	Repair Military Power Supplies	UNIT	AN	1
Subject Area 4 Communications Security (COMSEC)				
091-94E-1065	Repair Fill Devices (*) SKL	AIT	OT	1
091-94E-1069	Maintain the KVG-72(*)	AIT	OT	1
Subject Area 5 Security				
091-94E-1030	Implement COMSEC Security Protocol	AIT	OT	1
Skill Level SL2				
Subject Area 6 Maintenance Administration				
091-94E-2002	Perform Tech Inspection of Radio/CCI Equipment	UNIT	AN	2
091-94E-2003	Verify Repair of Radio/CCI Equipment	UNIT	AN	2
091-94E-2001	React to COMSEC Insecurity	UNIT	AN	2

This page intentionally left blank.

CHAPTER 3

MOS/Skill Level Tasks

Skill Level SL1
Subject Area 1: Receivers-Transmitters

091-94E-1021
Repair Receiver-Transmitter RT-1523(*)(C)/U

WARNING

- HIGH VOLTAGE is present during testing and troubleshooting of SINCGARS Components. DEATH ON CONTACT can result, so observe the following safety precautions: If at all possible, work on the equipment only when another person is nearby who is competent in CARDIOPULMONARY RESUSCITATION (CPR).

- DO NOT BE MISLED by the terms "low voltage" and "low potential". Voltages/potentials as low as 50 volts can cause DEATH under certain conditions.

- Remove or tape all personal metal objects (e.g., watches, rings, and medallions) before working on C−E equipment. For Artificial Respiration, refer to FM 21-11.

Conditions: In an operational environment, a customer unit has opened a work order for a faulty RT-1523(*) C/U. After receiving the open Work Order, your section Sergeant assigns the job to you. At your workstation you have the following items: Military Power Supply; Radio Test Set, AN/GRM-122; Interconnecting Group, ON-373B; Tool Kit, TK-105(*)/G; TM 11-5820-890-30P-1; TM 11-5820-890-30P-2; TM 11-5820-890-30P-3; DA Form 2404, Equipment Inspection And Maintenance Worksheet; DA Form 2407, Maintenance Request; DA Pam 750-8, The Army Maintenance Management System (TAMMS) Users Manual and Local Standard Operation Procedure (SOP).
NOTE: If any of the above equipment is obsolete or not available, use equivalent equipment.

Standards: 1. Repaired the RT-1523(*) C/U in accordance with applicable technical manual. 2. Completed all maintenance forms and records in accordance with DA Pam 750-8 without error. 3. Ensured all safety precautions are observed without violation.

Special Condition: None
Special Standards: None
Special Equipment: None

Cue: Your ELM shop just received a faulty RT-1523(*)C/U. Your Section Sergeant has assigned the work order to you for repair.

Performance Steps

1. Obtain required tools and test equipment. (TM 11-5820-890-30P-1)

2. Fill appropriate blocks on DA Form 2407 in accordance with DA PAM 750-8.

3. Perform Visual inspection.

    a. Check control knobs and RT pin connectors.

    b. Repair any fault that would cause the operational check to fail.

4. Perform Operational Check. (TM 11-5820-890-30P-1)

5. Skip to PS# 10 if RT passes operational check, continue to next step if RT fails.

6. Perform troubleshooting procedures. (TM 11-5820-890-30P-1)

7. Identify the defective module(s) or component(s).

8. Replace the defective module(s) or component(s).

9. Verify repair, repeat Operational Check PS# 4.

10. Finalize appropriate blocks on DA Form 2407 in accordance with DA PAM 750-8.

11. Tag defective part(s) for turn-in. (DA PAM 750-8)

12. Notify section supervisor upon completion of task.

Evaluation Preparation:
None

Performance Measures

		GO	NO-GO
1.	Obtained required tools and test equipment. (TM 11-5820-890-30P-1).	_____	_____
2.	Filled appropriate blocks on DA Form 2407 in accordance with DA PAM 750-8.	_____	_____
3.	Performed Visual inspection, corrected deficiencies.	_____	_____
4.	Performed Operational Check. (TM 11-5820-890-30P-1).	_____	_____
5.	Skipped to PS# 10 if RT passed operational check, or continued to next step if RT failed.	_____	_____
6.	Performed troubleshooting procedures. (TM 11-5820-890-30P-1).	_____	_____
7.	Identified the defective module(s) or component(s).	_____	_____

29 July 2014

	GO	NO-GO

Performance Measures

8. Replaced the defective module(s) or component(s). _____ _____

9. Repeated Operational Check PS#4 to verify repair. _____ _____

10. Finalized appropriate blocks on maintenance DA Form 2407 in accordance with DA PAM 750-8. _____ _____

11. Tagged defective part(s) for turn-in. (DA PAM 750-8). _____ _____

12. Notified section supervisor when task complete. _____ _____

Evaluation Guidance: None

References
Required
DA Form 2404
DA Form 2407
DA PAM 750-8
TM 11-5820-890-30P-1
TM 11-5820-890-30P-2
TM 11-5820-890-30P-3

091-94E-1703
Repair Radio Set AN/PRC-90(*)

CAUTION

Operation of the AN/PRC-90 without adequate RF shielding is prohibited except during a bona fide emergency situation. Keep the function switch in the OFF position at all times when not in emergency use and operate the VOL control in the minimum position during voice transmissions. Failure to observe these precautions will shorten battery life and could result in equipment failure or disrupt actual search missions. If the unit is issued in a sealed container, do not break the seal until the emergency conditions have stabilized.

Conditions: In an operational environment, an operator has turned in a non-mission capable AN/PRC-90(*) to your Shop. Your supervisor has directed you to perform a serviceability inspection of the radio set, given the following: Radio Set, AN/PRC-90(*); Radio Test set, AN/GRM-114A; Counter, Electronic, AN/USM-459; Test Set, Radio,TS-24B; TM 1-1680-377-13&P-2; TM 11-5820-1049-12; TM 11-5820-1049-30; TM 11-6625-3300-10; DA Form 2404, Equipment Inspection And Maintenance Worksheet; DA Form 2407, Maintenance Request; DA Pam 750-8, The Army Maintenance Management System (TAMMS) Users Manual; TB 385-4, Safety Requirements For Maintenance Of Electrical And Electronic Equipmet and Local Standard Operating Procedure (SOP).

NOTE: If any of the above equipment is obsolete or not available, use equivalent equipment.

Standards: Performed serviceability inspection of the AN/PRC-90(*) in accordance with TM 1-1680-377-13&P-2, TM 11-5820-1049-30.

Special Condition: None
Special Standards: None
Special Equipment: None

Cue: Your supervisor has directed you to perform a serviceability inspection of the AN/PRC-90(*).

Note: None

Performance Steps

1. Obtain required tools and test equipment in accordance with TM 1-1680-377-13&P-2.

2. Complete appropriate blocks on DA Form 2407 in accordance with DA PAM 750-8.

3. Perform visual inspection in accordance with TM 1-1680-377-13&P-2.

    a. Chassis

    b. Connectors / Cables

    c. Antenna

d. Battery

4. Set up test equipment in accordance with TM 1-1680-377-13&P-2.

5. Verify the symptom(s): perform operational check in accordance with TM 1-1680-377-13&P-.

    a. Self test

    b. Output tests

    c. Signal tests

6. Proceed to PS#12 if AN/PRC90 passes operational check: if not, perform troubleshooting procedures.

7. Troubleshoot the maintenance equipment in accordance with TM 1-1680-377-13&P-2.

8. Identify the defective circuit card(s) or component(s).

9. Replace the defective circuit(s) or component(s).

10. Verify the repair.

11. Perform operational check in accordance with TM 1-1680-377-13&P-2.

12. Complete DA Form 2407 in accordance with DA PAM 750-8.

13. Tag defective part(s) for turn in, in accordance with DA PAM 750-8.

14. Request final inspection upon completion of task (Refer to Local SOP).

Evaluation Preparation:
Ensure all items required in the condition statement (or appropriate substitutions) are on hand and all safety requirements are met.

		GO	NO-GO
Performance Measures			
1.	Obtained required tools and test equipment.	_____	_____
2.	Completed appropriate blocks on DA Form 2407 in accordance with DA PAM 750-8.	_____	_____
3.	Performed visual inspection.	_____	_____
4.	Set up test equipment.	_____	_____
5.	Verified symptom(s),performed operational check.	_____	_____
6.	Proceed to PS#12 if AN/PRC-90 passed operational check: if not, performed troubleshooting procedures.	_____	_____

	GO	NO-GO
Performance Measures		

7. Performed troubleshooting procedures. _____ _____

8. Identified the defective circuit card(s) or component(s). _____ _____

9. Replaced the defective circuit(s) or component(s). _____ _____

10. Verified the repair. _____ _____

11. Performed operational check. _____ _____

12. Completed maintenance forms. _____ _____

13. Tagged defective part(s) for turn in. _____ _____

14. Requested final inspection upon completion of task. (Refer to Local SOP) _____ _____

Evaluation Guidance: Score the Soldier GO if all performance measures are passed (P). Score the Soldier NO-GO if any performance measure is failed (F). If the Soldier fails any performance measure, show what was done wrong and how to do it correctly.

References
Required
DA FORM 2404
DA Form 2407
DA PAM 750-8
TB 385-4
TM 1-1680-377-13&P-2
TM 11-5820-1049-12
TM 11-5820-1049-30
TM 11-6625-3300-10

091-94E-1402
Repair Receiver-Transmitter RT-(*)/ARC-164(V)(*)

WARNING

Radio frequency electromagnetic radiation can cause fatal internal bums. It can literally "cook" internal organs and flesh. DO NOT touch or stand within 30 inches of antenna when the RT is keyed. If you feel the slightest warming effect while near this equipment, MOVE AWAY QUICKLY!!

HIGH VOLTAGE is used in the radio. DEATH ON CONTACT can result. So observe the following safety precautions:

- If at all possible, work on the equipment only when another person is nearby. That person should be competent in CARDIOPULMONARY RESUSCITATION (CPR).

- DO NOT BE MISLED by the terms "low voltage"and "low potential". Voltages and potentials as low as 50 volts can cause death.

- Remove or tape all your exposed personal metal objects when working on C-E equipment.

CAUTION

Devices such as CMOS, INOS, -VXOS, HEOS, thin-film resistors PNOS, and MSOFET used in many equipments can be damaged by static voltages present in most repair facilities. Most of the components contain internal gate protection circuits that are partially effective, but sound maintenance practice and the cost of equipment failure in time and money dictate careful handling of all electrostatic sensitive components.

Volume levels at the handset/headset/earphone/loudspeaker must be adjusted to the minimum levels required for operation. The volume control should be adjusted from the minimum position up to a comfortable level. Prolonged excessive volume will lead to hearing loss.

Conditions: In an operational environment, a non-mission capable RT-(*)/ARC-164(V) has been turned in to your Shop for repair. Your supervisor has directed you to restore the receiver transmitter to operational status, given the following: Receiver Transmitter RT-(*)/ARC-164(V); Wattmeter AN/URM-120; Signal Generator SG-1112(V)1/U; RF Voltmeter ME-426/U; Headset-Microphone H-157A/AIC; Oscilloscope AN/USM-488; Digital Multimeter AN/USM-486; Test Facilities Kit MK-994A/AR; AN/GRM-122; Distortion Analyzer HP-399A; Variable Attenuator CN-318/G; Power Supply HP-6433B; Radio Set Control C-9682A/ARC-164(V)(*); Tool Kit TK-105/G; Mixer HP 10514A CB-2343U; Attenuator, NARDA 766-30, 30-dB; static work station, NSN 4940-01-087-3458; TM 11-5821-356-23, TM 11-6625-3300-10, applicable repair parts; DA Form 2404, Equipment Inspection And Maintenance Worksheet; DA Form 2407, Maintenance Request; DA Pam 750-8, The Army Maintenance Management System (TAMMS) Users

Manual; TB 385-4, Safety Requirements For Maintenance Of Electrical And Electronic Equipmet and Local Standard Operating Procedure (SOP).

NOTE: If any of the above equipment is obsolete or not available, use equivalent equipment.

Standards: Restore the receiver-transmitter to an operational status in accordance with references listed in the performance measures.

Special Condition: None
Special Standards: None
Special Equipment: None

Cue: None

Note: None

Performance Steps

1. Obtain required tools and test equipment. (TM 11-6625-3300-10)

2. Complete appropriate blocks on DA Form 2407. (DA PAM 750-8)

3. Perform visual inspection. (TM 11-6625-3300-10)

4. Set up test equipment. (TM 11-6625-3300-10.)

5. Verify the symptom(s), perform operational tests.

6. Proceed to PS# 12 if Unit Under Test (UUT) passes operational tests. If UUT fails, start troubleshooting PS #7.

7. Perform troubleshooting procedures. (TM 11-6625-3300-10)

8. Identify the defective circuit card(s) or component(s).

9. Replace the defective circuit card(s) or component(s).

10. Verify the repair.

11. Perform operational tests. (TM 11-6625-3300-10)

12. Complete DA Form 2407. (DA PAM 750-8)

13. Tag defective part(s) for turn in. (DA PAM 750-8)

14. Request final inspection upon completion of task. (Refer to local SOP)

Evaluation Preparation:

Ensure all items required in the condition statement (or appropriate substitutions) are on hand and all safety requirements are met.

	Performance Measures	GO	NO-GO
1.	Obtained required tools and test equipment.	____	____
2.	Completed appropriate blocks on DA Form 2407.	____	____
3.	Performed visual inspection.	____	____
4.	Set up test equipment.	____	____
5.	Verified the symptom(s), performed operational tests.	____	____
6.	Proceeded to PS# 12 if Unit Under Test(UUT) passed operational tests or continued to PS #7 if UUT failed.	____	____
7.	Perform troubleshooting procedures.	____	____
8.	Identified defective circuit card(s) or component(s).	____	____
9.	Replaced defective circuit card(s) or component(s).	____	____
10.	Verified the repair.	____	____
11.	Perform operational tests.	____	____
12.	Completed DA 2407. (Refer to DA Pam 750-8.)	____	____
13.	Tagged defective part(s) for turn in.	____	____
14.	Requested final inspection. (Refer to local SOP.)	____	____

Evaluation Guidance: Score the soldier GO if all performance measures are passed. Score the soldier NO-GO if any performance measure is failed. If the soldier fails any performance measure, show what was done wrong and how to do it correctly.

References
Required
DA Form 2404
DA Form 2407
DA PAM 750-8
TB 385-4
TM 11-5821-356-23
TM 11-6625-3300-10

091-94E-1059
Repair AN/PSC-5(*)

WARNING

- Use of the AN/PSC-5 in the AM or FM Line-Of-Sight (LOS) modes cannot expose the user to nonionizing
radiation greater than the whole-body or partial-body limits. Physical contact with any nearby metallic objects may cause a RF shock or burn and shall therefore be avoided. Do not use the antenna if
the sheath covering is damaged or removed because contact with the internal metallic parts of the antenna can cause a RF shock or burn.

- Volume levels at the handset/headset/earphone/loudspeaker must be adjusted to the minimum levels required for operation. The volume control should be adjusted from the minimum position up to a
comfortable level. Prolonged excessive volume will lead to hearing loss.

Conditions: In an operational environment, a unit has submitted for repair a faulty AN/PSC-5(*) to your maintenance shop. Your supervisor has directed you to perform the repair. At your workstation you have the following: Digital Multimeter, AN/PSM-45A; Modulation Meter , ME-505A; Power Meter , AN/USM-491; Handset, H-250( )/U; Key Fill Device; Tool Kit, TK-105(*)/G and power supply, TM 11-5820-1130-30&P; DA Form 2404, Equipment Inspection And Maintenance Worksheet; DA Form 2407, Maintenance Request; DA Pam 750-8, The Army Maintenance Management System (TAMMS) Users Manual; TB 385-4, Safety Requirements For Maintenance Of Electrical And Electronic Equipmet and Local Standard Operating Procedure (SOP).

NOTE: Equivalent tools, test equipment, and accessories may be substituted with like items.

Standards: 1. Repaired the AN/PSC-5(*) in accordance with TM 11-5820-1130-30&P.
2. Completed maintenance forms and records in accordance with DA Pam 750-8.
3. Ensured all safety precautions are observed without violation.

Special Condition: None
Special Standards: None
Special Equipment: None

Cue: faulty AN/PSC-5(*) has been submitted to your repair shop. Your supervisor has directed you to perform the repair .

Note: TM 11-5820-1130-30&P is used for all references unless otherwise noted.

Performance Steps

1. Obtain required tools and test equipment. (Ch. 4.1)

2. Fill appropriate blocks on DA Form 2407 in accordance with DA PAM 750-8.

3. Perform visual inspection. (Ch. 4.3)

4. Conduct performance test. (Ch. 4.4)

5. Isolate fault by using the Fault Isolation Table. (Ch. 4.5)

6. Identify the defective module(s) or component(s).

7. Replace the defective module(s) or component(s).

8. Conduct performance test to verify repair. (Ch 4.5.2)

9. Finalize appropriate blocks on DA Form 2407 in accordance with DA PAM 750-8.

10. Tag defective part(s) for turn-in in accordance with DA PAM 750-8.

11. Notify section supervisor upon completion of task.

Evaluation Preparation:
Ensure all items required in the condition statement (or appropriate substitutions) are on hand and all safety requirements are met.

	Performance Measures	GO	NO-GO
1.	Obtained required tools and test equipment.	____	____
2.	Filled appropriate blocks on DA Form 2047.	____	____
3.	Performed visual inspection.	____	____
4.	Conducted performance test.	____	____
5.	Isolated fault by using the Fault Isolation Table.	____	____
6.	Identified the defective module(s) or component(s).	____	____
7.	Replaced the defective module(s) or component(s).	____	____
8.	Conducted performance test.	____	____
9.	Finalized appropriate blocks on DA Form 2407.	____	____
10.	Tagged defective part(s) for turn-in.	____	____
11.	Notified section supervisor upon completion of task.	____	____

Evaluation Guidance: Score the Soldier GO if all performance measures are passed (P). Score the Soldier NO-GO if any performance measure is failed (F). If the Soldier fails any performance measure, show what was done wrong and how to do it correctly.

References
Required
DA Form 2404
DA Form 2407
DA PAM 750-8
TB 385-4
TM 11-5820-1130-30&P

091-94E-1067
Maintain RT-(*)/ARC-231(*)

WARNING

- NOT BE MISLED by the terms "low voltage" and "low potential". Voltages/potentials as low as 50 volts can cause DEATH under certain conditions.
- Remove or tape all personal metal objects (e.g., watches, rings, and medallions) before working on C–E equipment. For Artificial Respiration, refer to FM 21-11.
- Never work on electronic equipment unless there is another person nearby who is familiar with the operation and hazards of the equipment and who is competent in administering first aid. When the technicians are aided by operators, they must be warned about dangerous areas.
- Whenever possible, the power supply to the equipment must be shut off before beginning work on the equipment. Take particular care to ground every capacitor likely to hold a dangerous potential. When working inside the equipment, after the power has been turned off, always ground every part before touching it.

- Be careful not to contact high-voltage connections or 115 volt AC input connections when installing or operating this equipment.

- Whenever the nature of the operation permits, keep one hand away from the equipment to reduce the hazard of current flowing through the body.

CAUTION

This equipment contains parts and assemblies sensitive to damage by electrostatic discharge (ESD). Use ESD precautionary procedures when touching, removing or inserting printed circuit boards.

Conditions: In an operational environment, a user has submitted an inoperable AN/ARC-231 to your repair shop. Your supervisor has directed you to identify/verify the fault, and perform any authroized repair. At your workstation you have the following: AN/ARC-231(*); AN/GRM-122; Tool Kit TK-105/G; Static Work Station, NSN 4940-01-087-3458; TM 11-6625-3300-10; DA Form 2404, Equipment Inspection and Maintenance Worksheet; DA Form 2407, Maintenance Request; DA Pam 750-8, The Army Maintenance Management System (TAMMS) Users Manual; TB 385-4, Safety Requirements for Maintenance of Electrical and Electronic Equipment and Local Standard Operating Procedure (SOP).

NOTE: Equivalent tools, test equipment, and accessories may be substituted with like items.

Standards: Test the AN/ARC-231(*) in accordance with TM 11-6625-3300-10. Complete maintenance forms and records in accordance with DA Pam 750-8. Ensure all safety precautions are observed without violation.

Special Condition: None

Special Standards: None

Special Equipment: None

Cue: Your Supervisor directs you to indentify/verify the fault an inoperable AN/ARC-231(*).

Note: None

Performance Steps

1. Obtain required tools and test equipment. (TM 11-6625-3300-10)

2. Complete appropriate blocks on DA Form 2407. (DA PAM 750-8)

3. Perform visual inspection.

4. Connect test equipment. (TM 11-6625-3300-10)

5. Perform Operational Check. If check passes proceed to step 8, if check fails, continue to PS #6.

6. Identify/verify equipment fault.

Note: Repair is not currently authorized for AN/ARC-231. If a fault is found, annotate fault on DA Form 2404 and DA Form 2407 and prepare radio for turn-in.

7. Tag defective radio for turn in.

8. Complete DA Form 2407. (DA PAM 750-8)

9. Request final inspection. (Refer to local SOP)

Evaluation Preparation:
Ensure all items required in the condition statement (or appropriate substitutions) are on hand and all safety requirements are met.

Performance Measures	GO	NO-GO
1. Obtained required tools and test equipment. (TM 11-6625-3300-10)	_____	_____
2. Completed appropriate blocks on DA Form 2407. (DA PAM 750-8)	_____	_____
3. Performed visual inspection.	_____	_____
4. Connected test equipment. (TM 11-6625-3300-10)	_____	_____
5. Performed Operational Check. If check passed proceeded to step 8, if check failed, continued to PS #6.	_____	_____

Performance Measures	GO	NO-GO
6. Identified/verified equipment fault.	_____	_____
7. Tagged defective radio for turn in.	_____	_____
8. Complete DA Form 2407. (DA PAM 750-8).	_____	_____
9. Request final inspection. (Refer to local SOP)	_____	_____

Evaluation Guidance: Score the Soldier GO if all performance measures are passed (P). Score the Soldier NO-GO if any performance measure is failed (F). If the Soldier fails any performance measure, show what was done wrong and how to do it correctly.

References
Required
DA Form 2404
DA Form 2407
DA Pam 750-8
TB 385-4
TM 11-6625-3300-10

091-94E-1068
Maintain High Frequency (HF) Radios

WARNING

Use of the AN/PSC-5 in the AM or FM Line-Of-Sight (LOS) modes cannot expose the user to nonionizing radiation greater than the whole-body or partial-body limits. Physical contact with any nearby metallic objects may cause a RF shock or burn and shall therefore be avoided. Do not use the antenna if the sheath covering is damaged or removed because contact with the internal metallic parts of the antenna can cause a RF shock or burn.

Conditions: In an operational environment, your supervisor has directed you to troubleshoot and repair a High Frequency (HF) radio that was submitted to your ELM shop this morning. At your work station you have the following items: Digital Multimeter, AN/PSM-45A; Modulation Meter, ME-505A/U; Power Meter with Sensor, AN/USM-491; Attenuator, 20 dB; Handset, H-250( )/U; Key Fill Device; TK-105(*)/G; TM 11-5820-1130-30&P; TM 11-5820-1501-13&P; TB 11-5820-1130-30; DA Form 2404, Equipment Inspection And Maintenance Worksheet; DA Form 2407, Maintenance Request; DA Pam 750-8, The Army Maintenance Management System (TAMMS) Users Manual; TB 385-4, Safety Requirements For Maintenance Of Electrical And Electronic Equipmet and Local Standard Operating Procedure (SOP).

NOTE: If any of the above equipment is obsolete or not available, use equivalent equipment.

Standards: Maintain the HF Radios in accordance with applicable technical manuals and be fully mission capable when the task is completed. Complete all maintenance forms and records in accordance with DA Pam 750-8 without error. Ensure all safety precautions are observed without violation

Special Condition: None
Special Standards: None
Special Equipment: None

Cue Your Supervisor has directed you to troubleshoot and repair an HF radio.

Note: DO NOT USE FREQUENCIES NOT ASSIGNED BY HIGHER COMMAND. Radio Set AN/PSC-5 contains the capability of extended frequency operations from 30 to 399.995 MHz. This feature is included to provide maximum capability for communications in a global environment for US, Federal, and allied Forces. Inclusion of this feature does not include authorization for indiscriminate use. The allocation of radio frequencies is governed by worldwide treaties, military, and civilian laws. Inappropriate or uncoordinated use of this extended range may be viewed as a violation of such laws or treaties and may make you personally liable for criminal offenses or fines associated with your actions. You are cautioned that use of the extended frequency range beyond the traditional military bands should be carefully coordinated and approved. Failure to do so could cause unwanted interference with commercial or public service traffic and will make you liable under the laws of the respective country you are operating in.

Performance Steps

1. Obtain required tools and test equipment.

2. Complete appropriate blocks on DA Form 2407. (DA PAM 750-8)

3. Perform visual inspection.

4. Set up test equipment.

5. Verify the symptom(s), perform operational tests.

6. Proceed to PS# 12 if Unit Under Test (UUT) passes operational tests. If UUT fails, start troubleshooting PS #7.

7. Perform troubleshooting procedures.

8. Identify the defective circuit card(s) or component(s).

9. Replace the defective circuit card(s) or component(s).

10. Verify the repair.

11. Perform operational tests, restart at PS# 5.

12. Complete DA Form 2407. (DA PAM 750-8)

13. Tag defective part(s) for turn in. (DA PAM 750-8)

14. Request final inspection upon completion of task. (Refer to local SOP)

Evaluation Preparation:
Ensure all items required in the condition statement (or appropriate substitutions) are on hand and all safety requirements are met.

Performance Measures

		GO	NO-GO
1.	Obtained required tools and test equipment.	____	____
2.	Completed appropriate blocks on DA Form 2407.	____	____
3.	Performed visual inspection.	____	____
4.	Set up test equipment.	____	____
5.	Verified the symptom(s), performed operational tests.	____	____
6.	Proceeded to PS# 12 if Unit Under Test(UUT) passed operational tests or continued to PS #7 if UUT failed.	____	____

	GO	NO-GO

Performance Measures

7. Perform troubleshooting procedures. _____ _____

8. Identified defective circuit card(s) or component(s). _____ _____

9. Replaced defective circuit card(s) or component(s). _____ _____

10. Verified the repair. _____ _____

11. Performed operational tests. _____ _____

12. Completed DA Form 2407. (Refer to DA Pam 750-8.) _____ _____

13. Tagged defective part(s) for turn in. _____ _____

14. Requested final inspection. (Refer to local SOP) _____ _____

Evaluation Guidance: Score the soldier GO if all performance measures are passed. Score the soldier NO-GO if any performance measure is failed. If the soldier fails any performance measure, show what was done wrong and how to do it correctly.

References
Required
DA Form 2404
DA Form 2407
DA Pam 750-8
TB 11-5820-1130-30
TB 385-4
TM 11-5820-1130-30&P
TM 11-5820-1501-13&P

091-94E-1302
Repair Receiver-Transmitter RT-(*)/ARC-186(V)(*)

DANGER

DEATH ON CONTACT may result if personnel fail to observe safety precautions.

Never work on electronic equipment unless there is another person nearby who is familiar with the operation and hazards of the equipment and who is competent in administering first aid. When the technicians are aided by operators, they must be warned about dangerous areas.

Whenever possible, the power supply to the equipment must be shut off before beginning work on the equipment. Take particular care to ground every capacitor likely to hold a dangerous potential. When working inside the equipment, after the power has been turned off, always ground every part before touching it.

Be careful not to contact high-voltage connections or 115 volt ac input connections when installing or operating this equipment. Whenever the nature of the operation permits, keep one hand away from the equipment to reduce the hazard of current flowing through the body.

WARNING

Do not be misled by the term "low voltage." Potentials as low as 50 volts may cause death under adverse conditions.

Conditions: In an operational environment, a non-mission capable RT-(*)/ARC-186(V) has been turned in to your Shop. Your supervisor has directed you to restore the receiver-transmitter to operational status, given the following: Receiver-Transmitter RT-(*)/ARC-186(V); Power Supply PP-1104(*); Signal Generator SG-1207/U; Digital Multimeter AN/USM-486; Headset-Microphone H-157A/AIC; Attenuators, 6-dB and 30-dB; static work station, NSN 4940-01-087-3458; Tool Kit TK-105A/G; applicable repair parts; TM 11-5821-318-30; TM 11-5821-318-30P; TM 11-6625-3300-10; DA Form 2404, Equipment Inspection And Maintenance Worksheet; DA Form 2407, Maintenance Request; DA Pam 750-8, The Army Maintenance Management System (TAMMS) Users Manual; TB 385-4, Safety Requirements For Maintenance Of Electrical And Electronic Equipmet and Local Standard Operating Procedure (SOP).

NOTE: If any of the above equipment is obsolete or not available, use equivalent equipment.

Standards: Restore the receiver-transmitter to operational status in accordance with references listed in the performance measures.

Special Condition: None
Special Standards: None
Special Equipment: None

Cue: None

Note: None

Performance Steps

1. Obtain required tools and test equipment in accordance with TM 11-5821-318-30.

2. Complete appropriate blocks on DA Form 2407. (DA PAM 750-8)

3. Perform visual inspection.

4. Connect test equipment.

5. Perform operational check.

6. Proceed to PS #12 if Radio Control Set passes operational check, if not continue to PS #7.

7. Perform troubleshooting procedures.

8. Identify the defective module(s), circuit card(s), or component(s).

9. Replace the defective module(s), circuit card(s), or component(s).

10. Verify the repair with QA/QC.

11. Repeat operational Check PS #5.

12. Complete DA Form 2407. (Refer to DA Pam 750-8)

13. Tag defective part(s) for turn in.

14. Request final inspection. (Refer to local SOP)

Evaluation Preparation: None

Performance Measures	GO	NO-GO
1. Obtained the required tools and test equipment.	____	____
2. Completed appropriate blocks on DA Form 2407.	____	____
3. Performed visual inspection.	____	____
4. Connected test equipment.	____	____
5. Performed operational check.	____	____
6. Proceeded to PM 12 if radio passed operational check.	____	____

29 July 2014

	GO	NO-GO
Performance Measures		

7. Performed troubleshooting procedures. _____ _____

8. Identified the defective part(s). _____ _____

9. Replaced the defective part(s). _____ _____

10. Repair verified by QA/QC. _____ _____

11. Repeated operational Check PS #5. _____ _____

12. Completed DA Form 2407. _____ _____

13. Tagged defective part(s) for turn in. _____ _____

14. Requested final inspection. (Refer to local SOP) _____ _____

Evaluation Guidance: Score the Soldier a Go if all performance measures are passed. Score the Soldier a NO-GO if any performance measure is failed. If the soldier fails any performance measure, show what was done wrong and how to do it correctly.

References
Required
DA Form 2404
DA Form 2407
DA PAM 750-8
TB 385-4
TM 11-5821-318-30
TM 11-5821-318-30P
TM 11-6625-3300-10

091-94E-1202
Repair Receiver-Transmitter RT-(*)/ARC-201(V)(*)

WARNING

RF ENERGY may be present near the antenna during transmission. DO NOT touch or stand within 30 inches of antenna when the RT is keyed.

HIGH VOLTAGE is used in the radio. DEATH ON CONTACT can result. Observe the following safety precautions:

- If at all possible, work on the equipment only when another person is nearby. That person should be competent in CARDIOPULMONARY RESUSCITATION (CPR).

- DO NOT BE MISLED by the terms "low voltage"and "low potential". Voltages and potentials as low as 50 volts can cause death.

- Remove or tape all your exposed personal metal objects when working on C-E equipment.

CAUTION

Failure to observe all precautions when working with electronic equipment can cause permanent damage to the electrostatic sensitive device. This damage can cause the device to fail immediately or at a later date when exposed to an adverse environment.

Conditions: In an operational environment, an RT- (*)/ARC-201(V) (*) and a DA Form 2407, Maintenance Request have been turned in to your Shop. Your supervisor has directed that you restore the RT to operational status, given the following: Receiver Transmitter RT-(*)/ARC-201(V)(*); AN/GRM-122; Tool Kit TK-105/G; applicable repair parts; Static Work Station, NSN 4940-01-087-3458; TM 11-5821-333-13&P1; TM 11-5821-333-13&P2; DA Form 2404, Equipment Inspection And Maintenance Worksheet; DA Form 2407; DA Pam 750-8, The Army Maintenance Management System (TAMMS) Users Manual; TB 385-4, Safety Requirements For Maintenance Of Electrical And Electronic Equipmet and Local Standard Operating Procedure (SOP).

NOTE: If any of the above equipment is not available, use equivalent equipment.

Standards: Restore the RT to operational status in accordance with the Technical manual and the references listed in the performance measures.

Special Condition: None
Special Standards: None
Special Equipment: None

Cue: None

Note: None

Performance Steps

1. Obtain required tools and test equipment. (TM 11-5821-333-13&P1)

2. Complete appropriate blocks on DA Form 2407. (DA PAM 750-8)

3. Perform visual inspection.

4. Perform Safe to turn on check.

5. Connect test equipment. (TM 11-5821-333-13&P1)

6. Perform Operational Check. If check passes, proceed to step 12, if check fails, continue to PS #7.

7. Perform troubleshooting procedures.

8. Identify defective part.

9. Replace defective part.

10. Verify the repair with QA/QC.

11. Repeat operational Check PS #6.

12. Complete DA Form 2407. (DA PAM 750-8)

13. Tag defective part(s) for turn in.

14. Request final inspection. (Refer to local SOP)

Evaluation Preparation:
Ensure all items required in the condition statement (or appropriate substitutions) are on hand and all safety requirements are met.

	Performance Measures	**GO**	**NO-GO**
1.	Obtained required tools and test equipment.	_____	_____
2.	Completed appropriate blocks on DA Form 2407.	_____	_____
3.	Performed visual inspection.	_____	_____
4.	Performed safe to turn on check.	_____	_____
5.	Connected test equipment.	_____	_____
		_____	_____

	GO	NO-GO
Performance Measures		

6. Performed Operational Check. If check passed, proceeded to step 12, if check failed, continued to PS #7.

7. Performed troubleshooting procedures. _____ _____

8. Identified defective part. _____ _____

9. Replaced defective part. _____ _____

10. Verified the repair with QA/QC. _____ _____

11. Repeated operational Check PS #4. _____ _____

12. Completed DA Form 2407. _____ _____

13. Tagged defective part(s) for turn in. _____ _____

14. Requested final inspection. (Refer to local SOP) _____ _____

Evaluation Guidance: Score the Soldier a Go if all performance measures are passed. Score the Soldier a NO-GO if any performance measure is failed. If the Soldier fails any performance measure, show what was done wrong and how to do it correctly

References
Required
DA Form 2404
DA Form 2407
DA PAM 750-8
TB 385-4
TM 11-5821-333-13&P-1
TM 11-5821-333-13&P-2

091-94E-1702
Test the AN/PRC-112(*)

WARNING

Touching the antenna of the AN/PRC-112 Survival Radio with unprotected skin (hands, face, etc.), foreign metal objects or wet earth/foliage while transmitting or receiving will significantly degrade the signal, resulting in reduced performance of the radio.

DO NOT transmit on 121.5 MHz, 243.0 MHz, or 282.8 MHz unless under actual emergency conditions. Beacon transmission on 121.5 MHz or 243.0 MHz frequencies may result in your location by the enemy and significantly reduce battery life. The frequency 282.8 MHz is designated as a Search and Rescue frequency.

CAUTION

Ensure that the Radio Set is turned OFF before removing or installing the battery pack.

The radio interface pins at the top of the Program Loader KY-913/PRC-112 are connected directly to the battery pack when attached. The power pins are live. Keep the cover for this connector in place whenever the Program Loader is not attached to the Radio Set to prevent accidental damage to the battery pack.

DO NOT thrust pointed or sharp tools or instruments into the interior of the carton as damage to the equipment could occur.

Conditions: In an operational environment, a suspected faulty AN/PRC-112(*) is submitted for repair to your maintenance shop. Your supervisor directs you to test the faulty AN/PRC-112(*). At your workstation you have the following: Radio Set, AN/PRC-112(*); Radio Set, PLS AN/ARS-6(V); Test Set, TS-4360/AYD; Program Loader, KY-913/PRC-112; Test Set, AN/GRM-122; TM 1-1680-377-13&P-2; TM 11-5820-1037-13&P; DA Form 2404, Equipment Inspection And Maintenance Worksheet; DA Form 2407, Maintenance Request; DA Pam 750-8, The Army Maintenance Management System (TAMMS) Users Manual; TB 385-4, Safety Requirements For Maintenance Of Electrical And Electronic Equipmet and Local Standard Operating Procedure (SOP).

NOTE: If any of the above equipment is obsolete or not available, use equivalent equipment.

Standards: Tested the AN/PRC-112 in accordance with TM 1-1680-377-13&P-2 and TM 11-5820-1037-13&P.

Special Condition: None
Special Standards: None
Special Equipment: None

Cue: Your supervisor has directed you to test the AN/PRC-112(*) radio set.

Note: None

Performance Steps

1. Obtain required tools and test equipment. (TM 1-1680-377-13&P-2 WP 0213)

2. Complete appropriate blocks on DA Form 2407. (DA PAM 750-8)

3. Perform visual inspection.

4. Set up test equipment. (WP 0213)

5. Verify faults, Perform Operational Checks.

   a. Radio current test, programming test and transponder mode tests. (WP 0213 PG 00-3)

   b. Transmitter power, transmitter modulation percentage, receiver distortion and SINAD Tests. (WP 0214)

6. Complete DA Form 2407. (DA Pam 750-8 Ch. 3)

7. Request final inspection upon completion of task. (Refer to local SOP)

Evaluation Preparation:
Ensure all items required in the condition statement (or appropriate substitutions) are on hand and all safety requirements are met.

	GO	NO-GO
Performance Measures		
1. Obtained required tools and test equipment.	_____	_____
2. Completed appropriate blocks on DA Form 2407.	_____	_____
3. Performed visual inspection.	_____	_____
4. Set up test equipment in accordance with TM.	_____	_____
5. Performed operational checks.	_____	_____
6. Completed DA Form 2407.	_____	_____
7. Requested final inspection upon completion of task.	_____	_____

Evaluation Guidance: Score the Soldier GO if all performance measures are passed (P). Score the Soldier NO-GO if any performance measure is failed (F). If the Soldier fails any performance measure, show what was done wrong and how to do it correctly

References
Required
DA Form 2404

Required
DA Form 2407
DA PAM 750-8
TB 385-4
TM 11-5820-1037-13&P
TM 11-6625-3263-25

Subject Area 2: Auxiliary Equipment
091-94E-1102
Repair Communications System Control C-6533(*)/ARC

CAUTION

This equipment contains transistor circuits in the headset and microphone amplifiers and the protective device and filter assembly. If any test equipment item does not have an isolation transformer in its power supply circuit, connect one in the power input circuit.

Before using any multimeter to test transistors of transistor circuits, check the open-circuit voltage across the multimeter test leads. Do not use the multimeter if the open circuit voltage exceeds 1.5 volt. Also, since the Rxl range normally connects the multimeter internal battery directly across the test leads, the comparatively high current (50 ma or more) may damage the transistor under test. As a general rule, it is not recommended that the Rxl range of any multimeter be used when testing low power transistors.

Conditions: In an Operational Environment, an operator has turned in a non-mission capable C-6533(*)/ARC to your Shop. Your supervisor has directed you to restore the equipment to operational status in accordance with the Technical Manual. Your shop is equipped with the following items: Communications System Control C-6533(*)/ARC; Radio Test Set AN/GRM-122(*); Headset-Microphone H-157A/AIC; Resistor, 150-ohm, .5-watt, 5-percent; Resistor, 200-ohm, .5-watt, 5-percent; Power Supply PP-1104(*); Digital Multimeter PSM-45A; Tool Kit-TK-105A(G); applicable repair parts; TM 11-5895-1174-23; TM 11-5895-1174-23P; TM 11-6625-3300-10; DA Form 2404, Equipment Inspection And Maintenance Worksheet; DA Form 2407, Maintenance Request; DA Pam 750-8, The Army Maintenance Management System (TAMMS) Users Manual; TB 385-4, Safety Requirements For Maintenance Of Electrical And Electronic Equipmet and Local Standard Operating Procedure (SOP).

NOTE: If any of the above equipment is obsolete or not available, use equivalent equipment.

Standards: Restore the communications system control to operational status in accordance with the Technical manual and references listed in the performance measures.

Special Condition: None
Special Standards: None
Special Equipment: None

Cue: None

Note: None

Performance Steps

1. Obtain required tools and test equipment. (11-5895-1174-23 Para 3-5)

2. Complete appropriate blocks on DA Form 2407. (DA PAM 750-8)

3. Perform visual inspection.

4. Set up test equipment. (TM 11-5895-1174-23 Fig. 3-1)

5. Perform Basic Test. (TM 11-5895-1174-23 table 3-1)

6. If Control passes Basic Test, proceed to next step. If control fails refer to table 3-2 for troubleshooting.

7. If Control passes All Other Functions Test, proceed to PS #12.

8. Identify the defective circuit card(s) or component(s).

9. Replace the defective circuit card(s) or component(s).

10. Verify the repair.

11. Verify operational readiness by Performance Testing. (TM 11-5895-1174-23 Para. 3-24)

12. Complete DA Form 2407. (DA Pam 750-8)

13. Tag defective part(s) for turn in. (DA PAM 750-8)

14. Request final inspection upon completion of task. (Local SOP)

Evaluation Preparation:
Ensure all items required in the condition statement (or appropriate substitutions) are on hand and all safety requirements are met.

	Performance Measures	GO	NO-GO
1.	Obtained required tools and test equipment.	_____	_____
2.	Completed appropriate blocks on DA Form 2407.	_____	_____
3.	Performed visual inspection.	_____	_____
4.	Set up test equipment.	_____	_____
5.	Performed basic test.	_____	_____
6.	If Control passed Basic Test, proceeded to next step. If control failed refered to table 3-2 for troubleshooting.	_____	_____
		_____	_____

	GO	NO-GO

Performance Measures

7. If Control passed All Other Functions Test, proceed to PS #12.

8.	Identified the defective circuit card(s) or component(s).	____	____
9.	Replaced the defective circuit card(s) or component(s).	____	____
10.	Verified the repair.	____	____
11.	Verified operational readiness by Performance Testing.	____	____
12.	Completed DA Form 2407.	____	____
13.	Tagged defective part(s) for turn in.	____	____
14.	Requested final inspection.	____	____

Evaluation Guidance: Score the soldier GO if all performance measures are passed (P). Score the soldier NO-GO if any performance measure is failed (F). If the soldier fails any performance measure, show what was done wrong and how to do it correctly.

References
Required
DA Form 2404
DA Form 2407
DA PAM 750-8
TB 385-4
TM 11-5895-1174-23
TM 11-5895-1174-23P
TM 11-6625-3300-10

29 July 2014

091-94E-1006
Repair Control Monitor C-11291(*)/VRC

WARNING

Connect the test equipment setups only when directed, and with the power supply set to OFF. The large current capacity of the test power supply can cause personal injury. Verify the test equipment setup before turning the power supply ON.

CAUTION

Static electricity can cause degraded or catastrophic damage to electronic components. To prevent Electrostatic Discharge (ESD) when performing maintenance, use a grounded antistatic pad, wear a grounded wrist strap, and keep work area free of non-conductors.

Steps marked with HCP must be performed exactly as written. They are critical in maintaining the nuclear hardness of the Line Replaceable Unit. Seals must not be damaged and screws and nuts
must be torqued to the limits specified.

Conditions: You are in an operational environment, a non-mission capable C -11291(*)/VRC with DA Form 2407, Maintenance Request have been submitted to your ELM shop. Your supervisor has assigned the work order to you for repair. At your workstation you have the following items: Tool Set, TK-105(*)/G; Military Power Supply; Radio Test Set, AN/GRM 122; I nterconnecting Group, ON-373(*)/GRC; Repair Parts; TM 11-5820-890-30 ; TM 11-5820-890-30P-1; TM 11-5820-890-30P-2; TM 11-5820-890-30P-3; TM 11-6625-3300-10; DA Form 2404, Equipment Inspection And Maintenance Worksheet; DA Form 2407; DA Pam 750-8, The Army Maintenance Management System (TAMMS) Users Manual; TB 385-4, Safety Requirements For Maintenance Of Electrical And Electronic Equipmet and Local Standard Operating Procedure (SOP). NOTE: If any of the above equipment is obsolete or not available, use equivalent equipment.

NOTE: If any of the above equipment is obsolete or not available, use equivalent equipment.

Standards: Repaired the C-11291(*)/VRC in accordance with applicable technical manuals. Completed all maintenance forms and records in accordance with DA Pam 750-8.

Special Condition: None
Special Standards: None
Special Equipment: None

Cue: Your supervisor has directed you to repair a non-mission capable C-11291(*)/VRC submitted to your ELM shop.

Performance Steps

1. Obtain required tools and test equipment.

2. Complete appropriate blocks on maintenance forms. (DA Pam 750-8)

3. Set up test equipment.

4. Perform operational check.

5. Skip to PS #11 if Control Passes Operational checks, if tests fail continue to PS #6.

6. Perform Troubleshooting measures.

7. Identify the defective module(s) or component(s).

8. Replace the defective module(s) or component(s).

9. Repeat operational check PS #4 to verify repair.

10. Tag defective part(s) for turn-in. (DA Pam 750-8)

11. Finalize appropriate blocks on DA Form 2407. (DA Pam 750-8)

12. Notify section supervisor upon completion of task.

Evaluation Preparation:
Ensure all items required in the condition statement (or appropriate substitutions) are on hand and all safety requirements are met.

Performance Measures	**GO**	**NO-GO**
1. Obtained required tools, test equipment, and references.	_____	_____
2. Completed appropriate blocks on maintenance forms.	_____	_____
3. Set up test equipment in accordance with technical manual.	_____	_____
4. Performed operational check in accordance with TM.	_____	_____
5. Skipped to PS #11 if Control Passed Operational checks, if tests failed continued to PS #6.	_____	_____
6. Performed Troubleshooting measures.	_____	_____
7. Identified defective module(s) or component(s).	_____	_____
8. Replaced defective module(s) or component(s).	_____	_____

	GO	NO-GO

Performance Measures

9. Verified repair by through operational check.

10. Tagged defective parts for turn-in.

11. Completed appropriate blocks on maintenance forms.

12. Notified supervisor upon completion of task.

Evaluation Guidance: Score the soldier GO if all performance measures are passed (P). Scorethe soldier NO-GO if any performance measure is failed (F). Ifthe soldier failsany performance measure,show what was done wrong and how to do it correctly.

References
Required
DA Form 2404
DA Form 2407
DA PAM 750-8
TB 385-4
TM 11-5820-890-30
TM 11-5820-890-30P-1
TM 11-5820-890-30P-2
TM 11-5820-890-30P-3
TM 11-6625-3300-10

091-94E-1007
Repair Remote Control Unit C-11561 (C)/U

WARNING

Never work on electronic equipment unless there is another person nearby who is familiar with the operation and hazards of the equipment and who is competent in administering first aid. When the technicians are aided by operators, they must be warned about dangerous areas.

Whenever possible, the power supply to the equipment must be shut off before beginning work on the equipment. Take particular care to ground every capacitor likely to hold a dangerous potential. When working inside the equipment, after the power has been turned off, always ground every part before touching it. Be careful not to contact high−voltage connections or 115 volt AC input connections when installing or operating this equipment.

Whenever the nature of the operation permits, keep one hand away from the equipment to reduce the hazard of current flowing through the body.

DO NOT BE MISLED by the terms "low voltage" and "low potential". Voltages/potentials as low as 50 volts can cause DEATH under certain conditions.

CAUTION

This equipment contains parts sensitive to damage by electrostatic discharge (ESD).

Conditions: In an operational environment, your ELM shop has received a DA Form 2407, Maintenance Request for a non-mission capable C-11561(C)/U; your supervisor has directed you to perform the repair. At your workstation you have the following items; Military Power Supply; Interconnecting Group, ON-373B/GRC; Radio Test Set, AN/GRM 122; Tool Set, TK-105(*)/G; Repair Parts; TM 11-5820-890-30P; TM 11-5820-890-30P-1; TM 11-5820-890-30P-2; TM 11-5820-890-30P-3; DA Form 2404, Equipment Inspection And Maintenance Worksheet; DA Form 2407; DA Pam 750-8, The Army Maintenance Management System (TAMMS) Users Manual; TB 385-4, Safety Requirements For Maintenance Of Electrical And Electronic Equipmet and Local Standard Operating Procedure (SOP).

NOTE: If any of the above equipment is obsolete or not available, use equivalent equipment.

Standards: Repaired the C-11561(C)/U in accordance with TM 11-5820-890-30P. Completed all maintenance forms without error.

Special Condition: None
Special Standards: None
Special Equipment: None

Cue: Your supervisor has directed you to repair the faulty C-11561(C)/U submitted to your ELM shop.

Note: SINCGARS Technical Manual, TM 11-5820-890-30P-2, is comprised of 12 volumes; it covers the Operator, Field Maintenance, and Repair Parts and Special Tools List (RPSTL) for the SINCGARS Ground family of radios.

Performance Steps

1. Obtain required tools and test equipment.

2. Fill appropriate blocks on DA Form 2407. (DA Pam 750-8)

3. Perform visual inspection.

    a. Inspect external controls and connectors.

    b. Correct any deficiency that will impede operational checks.

4. Set up test equipment in accordance with TM.

5. Perform operational check.

6. Skip to PS# 11 if equipment passes operation check. Continue to PS# 7 if equipment fails.

7. Troubleshoot the equipment using the flowchart.

8. Identify the defective module(s) or component(s).

9. Replace the defective module(s) or component(s).

10. Repeat operational check to verify repair (PS# 5).

11. Finalize appropriate blocks on DA Form 2407. (DA Pam 750-8)

12. Tag defective part(s) for turn-in. (DA Pam 750-8)

13. Notify section supervisor upon completion of task.

Evaluation Preparation:
Ensure all items required in the condition statement (or appropriate substitutions) are on hand and all safety requirements are met.

		GO	NO-GO
Performance Measures			
1.	Obtained required tools and test equipment.	____	____
2.	Completed appropriate blocks on DA Form 2407.	____	____
3.	Performed visual inspection.	____	____

	GO	NO-GO
Performance Measures		

4. Set up test equipment in accordance with technical manual. _____ _____

5. Performed operational check. _____ _____

6. Skipped to PS# 11 if equipment passed operational check or continued to PS# 7 if equipment failed. _____ _____

7. Performed Troubleshooting procedures using the flowchart in TM 11-5820-890-30P-2. _____ _____

8. Identified the defective module(s) or component(s). _____ _____

9. Replaced the defective module(s) or component(s). _____ _____

10. Repeated operational check to verify repair. _____ _____

11. Finalized appropriate blocks on DA Form 2407. _____ _____

12. Tagged defective parts for turn-in. _____ _____

13. Notified supervisor upon completion of task. _____ _____

Evaluation Guidance: Score the soldier GO if all performance measures are passed (P). Score the soldier NO-GO if any performance measure is failed (F). If the soldier fails any performance measure, show what was done wrong and how to do it correctly.

References
Required
DA Form 2404
DA Form 2407
DA PAM 750-8
TB 385-4
TM 11-5820-890-30P
TM 11-5820-890-30P-1
TM 11-5820-890-30P-2
TM 11-5820-890-30P-3

091-94E-1005
Repair Amplifier-Adapter Vehicular AM-7239(*)/VRC

WARNING

HIGH VOLTAGE is present during testing and troubleshooting of AM-7239/VRC.
DEATH ON CONTACT can result, observe the following safety precautions:

If at all possible, work on the equipment only when another person is nearby who is competent in CARDIOPULMONARY RESUSCITATION (CPR)

DO NOT BE MISLED by the terms "low voltage" and "low potential". Voltages/potentials as low as 50 volts can cause DEATH under certain conditions.

Remove or tape all personal metal objects (e.g., watches, rings, and medallions) before working on C–E equipment.

Whenever the nature of the operation permits, keep one hand away from the equipment to reduce the hazard of current flowing through the body.

For Artificial Respiration, refer to FM 21-11.

CAUTION

This equipment contains parts sensitive to damage by electrostatic discharge (ESD).

Conditions: In an operational environment, a customer unit has submitted a DA Form 2407, Maintenance Request for a faulty AM-7239(*)/VRC. Upon receiving the open work order, your section Sergeant assigns the job to you for repair. At your workstation you have the following items: Military Power Supply; Radio Test Set, AN/GRM-122; Interconnecting Group, ON-373B; Tool Kit, TK-105(*)/G; TM 11-5820-890-30P-1; TM 11-5820-890-30P-2; TM 11-5820-890-30P-3; DA Form 2404, Equipment Inspection And Maintenance Worksheet; DA Form 2407; DA Pam 750-8, The Army Maintenance Management System (TAMMS) Users Manual; TB 385-4, Safety Requirements For Maintenance Of Electrical And Electronic Equipmet and Local Standard Operating Procedure (SOP). NOTE: If any of the above equipment is obsolete or not available, use equivalent equipment.

Standards: Repaired the AM-7239(*)/VRC in accordance with TM 11-5820-890-30P-2. Completed all maintenance forms and records in accordance with DA Pam 750-8 without error. Ensured all safety precautions are observed without violation.

Special Condition: None
Special Standards: None
Special Equipment: None

Cue: Your Section Sergeant has directed you to restore the faulty AM -7239(*)/VRC to a fully mission capable status in accordance with TM 11-5820-890-30P-2.

Performance Steps

1. Obtain required tools, test equipment.

2. Fill appropriate blocks on DA Form 2407. (DA PAM 750-8)

3. Perform visual inspection.

    a. Inspect.

        (1) Front panel connectors.

        (2) Rear panel connector.

        (3) Chassis.

    b. Repair any fault that would interfere with automated troubleshooting.

4. Set up test equipment.

5. Perform operational checks.

6. Skip to PS #11 if equipment passes operational check, if not, continue to next PS.

7. Troubleshoot equipment according to.

8. Identify defective module(s) or component(s).

9. Replace defective module(s) or component(s).

10. Repeat operational check PS #5, to verify repair.

11. Finalize appropriate blocks on DA Form 2407. (DA Pam 750-8)

12. Tag defective part(s) for turn-in. (DA Pam 750-8)

13. Notify supervisor upon completion of task.

Evaluation Preparation: None

Performance Measures	**GO**	**NO-GO**
1. Obtained required tools, test equipment.	_____	_____
2. Completed appropriate blocks on DA Form 2407.	_____	_____
3. Performed visual inspection.	_____	_____
4. Set up test equipment.	_____	_____
5. Performed operational checks.	_____	_____

Performance Measures	GO	NO-GO
6. Proceeded to PS #11 or PS #7 after operational check results.	_____	_____
7. Performed Troubleshooting according to TM.	_____	_____
8. Identified defective module(s) or component(s).	_____	_____
9. Replaced defective module(s) or component(s).	_____	_____
10. Verified repair through operational check.	_____	_____
11. Finalized appropriate blocks on DA Form 2407.	_____	_____
12. Tagged defective part(s) for turn-in.	_____	_____
13. Notified supervisor upon completion of task.	_____	_____

Evaluation Guidance: None

References
Required
DA Form 2404
DA Form 2407
DA PAM 750-8
TB 385-4
TM 11-5820-890-30P-1
TM 11-5820-890-30P-2
TM 11-5820-890-30P-3

Subject Area 3: Power Supplies
091-94E-1013
Repair Military Power Supplies

WARNING

High voltages and currents exist in this equipment. DO NOT TAKE CHANCES!

Be careful when working on the 115-volt or the 230-volt ac line connections. Serious injury or death can result from contact with these terminals.

To avoid possible electrical shock! Power Supply PP-6224/U should be used only with a 3-wire grounded ac power source, a 2-wire adapter must not be used.

Conditions: In an operational environment, a unit your ELM shop supports has turned in non-mission capable Military Power Supply (PP-6224(*)/U or PP-2953(*)/U) and DA Form 2407, Maintenance Request. Your shop foreman has assigned the work order to you for repair. Your work area has the following items available to complete the task; TK-105(*)/G; Multimeter TS-352B/U; Test Set, Transistor TS-1836/U; repair parts; TM 11-6130-233-12, TM 11-6130-233-24P, TM 11-6130-233-35, TM 11-6130-266-15, TM 11-6130-266-24P-2; DA Form 2404, Equipment Inspection And Maintenance Worksheet; DA Form 2407; DA Pam 750-8, The Army Maintenance Management System (TAMMS) Users Manual; TB 385-4, Safety Requirements For Maintenance Of Electrical And Electronic Equipmet and Local Standard Operating Procedure (SOP).

NOTE: If any of the above equipment is obsolete or not available, use equivalent equipment.

Standards: Repaired the power supply in accordance with the applicable technical manual. Correctly completed all maintenance form packet in accordance with DA Pam 750-8 Ch. 3.

Special Condition: None
Special Standards: None
Special Equipment: None

Cue: A non-mission capable Military Power Supply has been submitted to your ELM shop, your supervisor has directed you to perform the repair.

Note: None

Performance Steps

1. Obtain required tools and test equipment. (Refer to TM)

2. Fill appropriate blocks on DA Form 2407. (DA PAM 750-8 Ch. 3)

3. Perform visual inspection.

4. Set up test equipment.

5. Perform troubleshooting procedures.

6. Identify the defective module(s) or component(s).

7. Replace the defective module(s) or component(s).

8. Employ Power supply to verify repair.

9. Finalize appropriate blocks on DA Form 2407.

10. Tag defective part(s) for turn-in.

11. Notify section supervisor upon completion of task.

Evaluation Preparation:
Ensure all items required in the condition statement (or appropriate substitutions) are on hand and all safety requirements are met.

Performance Measures

		GO	NO-GO
1.	Obtained required tools, test equipment and references.	_____	_____
2.	Completed appropriate blocks on DA Form 2407.	_____	_____
3.	Performed visual inspection.	_____	_____
4.	Set up test equipment in accordance with TM.	_____	_____
5.	Performed troubleshooting procedures in accordance with TM.	_____	_____
6.	Identified the defective part(s).	_____	_____
7.	Replaced defective part(s) with operational ones.	_____	_____
8.	Employed Power supply to verify repair.	_____	_____
9.	Completed appropriate blocks on DA Form 2407.	_____	_____
10.	Tagged defective parts for turn-in.	_____	_____
11.	Notified supervisor upon completion of task.	_____	_____

Evaluation Guidance: Score the soldier GO if all performance measures are passed. Score the soldier NO-GO if any performance measure is failed. If the soldier fails any performance measure, show what was done wrong and how to do it correctly.

References
Required
DA Form 2404
DA Form 2407
DA Pam 750-8
TB 385-4
TM 11-6130-233-12
TM 11-6130-233-24P
TM 11-6130-266-24P-2
TM 11-6130-233-35
TM 11-6130-266-15

Subject Area 4: Communications Security (COMSEC)
091-94E-1065
Repair Fill Devices (*) SKL

WARNING

DO NOT USE BA-5372A/U (OR BA-1372/U) IN THE AN/CYZ-10. THESE BATTERIES CAN CAUSE A FIRE WHEN USED IN THE AN/CYZ-10. ALWAYS CHECK BATTERIES PRIOR TO INSERTING THEM INTO THE AN/CYZ-10.

Conditions: In an operational environment, a non-mission capable fill device has been submitted to your shop for repair. Your supervisor has tasked you to perform the job. At your workstation you have the following items: Fill Device, AN/CYZ-10 or Simple Key Loader, AN/PYQ-10; Laptop computer; Tool Kit TK-105(*)/G; Fill Cable; applicable repair parts; TM 11-5810-394-13&P; TM 11-5810-410-13&P; DA Form 2404, Equipment Inspection And Maintenance Worksheet; DA Form 2407, Maintenance Request; DA Pam 750-8, The Army Maintenance Management System (TAMMS) Users Manual; TB 385-4, Safety Requirements For Maintenance Of Electrical And Electronic Equipmet and Local Standard Operating Procedure (SOP). NOTE: If any of the above equipment is obsolete or not available, use equivalent equipment.

Standards: Repaired the fill device in accordance with applicable technical manuals. Completed maintenance forms in accordance with DA Pam 750-8 without error.

Special Condition: None
Special Standards: None
Special Equipment: None

Cue: None

Note: None

Performance Steps

1. Obtain required tools and test equipment.

2. Fill appropriate blocks on DA Form 2407. (DA PAM 750-8)

3. Perform visual inspection.

4. Check battery.

5. Perform operational test.

6. Analyze Bit results, if repair not authorized at Field Level, skip to PS 8. otherwise continue to PS 7.

7. Correct any malfunctions found.

NOTE: Repair is limited to the replacement of all external components only. Refer to Maintenance Allocation Chart (MAC) in the equipment TM for authorized repair.
ANCD: TM 11-5810-394-13&P Appendix B table 1.
SKL: TM 11-5810-410-13&P WP 43-1.

8. Complete appropriate blocks on DA Form 2407.

9. Notify supervisor of completion of task.

Evaluation Preparation:
Ensure all items required in the condition statement (or appropriate substitutions) are on hand and all safety requirements are met.

	GO	NO-GO
Performance Measures		
1. Obtained required tools, test equipment and references.	_____	_____
2. Completed appropriate blocks on DA Form 2407.	_____	_____
3. Performed visual inspection.	_____	_____
4. Checked battery.	_____	_____
5. Performed operational test.	_____	_____
6. Proceded to PM 7 or PM 8 after analyzing BIT results.	_____	_____
7. Corrected malfunctions found.	_____	_____
8. Completed appropriate blocks on DA Form 2407.	_____	_____
9. Notified supervisor of completion of task.	_____	_____

Evaluation Guidance: Score the Soldier GO if all performance measures are passed (P). Score the Soldier NO-GO if any performance measure is failed (F). If the Soldier fails any performance measure, show what was done wrong and how to do it correctly.

References
Required
DA Form 2404
DA Form 2407
DA PAM 750-8
TB 385-4
TM 11-5810-394-13&P
TM 11-5810-410-13&P

091-94E-1069
Maintain the KVG-72(*)

WARNING

DO NOT BE MISLED by the terms "low voltage" and "low potential". Voltages/potentials as low as 50 volts can cause DEATH under certain conditions. Remove or tape all personal metal objects (e.g., watches, rings, and medallions) before working on C–E equipment. For Artificial Respiration, refer to FM 21-11. Never work on electronic equipment unless there is another person nearby who is familiar with the operation and hazards of the equipment and who is competent in administering first aid. When the technicians are aided by operators, they must be warned about dangerous areas. Whenever possible, the power supply to the equipment must be shut off before beginning work on the equipment. Take particular care to ground every capacitor likely to hold a dangerous potential. When working inside the equipment, after the power has been turned off, always ground every part before touching it.

CAUTION

This equipment contains parts and assemblies sensitive to damage by electrostatic discharge (ESD). Use ESD precautionary procedures when touching, removing or inserting printed circuit boards.

Conditions: In an Operational Environment, a user submits an inoperable KVG-72 with Maintenance Request to your ELM Shop. After receiving the work order packet, your supervisor directs you to perform the troubleshooting. At your workstation you have the following items, Tool Kit, TK-105(*); Platform Encryption Device, KVG-72; Fault Verification Test Kit (FVTK); TB 11-7010-439-23, Field Testing And Assembly Instructions For Force XXI Battle Command Brigade And Below (FBCB2) Fault Verification Test Kit (KVTK) (NSN: 7010-01-557-0130); DA Form 2404, Equipment Inspection And Maintenance Worksheet; DA Form 2407, Maintenance Request; DA Pam 750-8, The Army Maintenance Management System (TAMMS) Users Manual; TB 385-4, Safety Requirements For Maintenance Of Electrical And Electronic Equipmet and Local Standard Operating Procedure (SOP). NOTE: If any of the above equipment is obsolete or not available, use equivalent equipment.

Standards: Maintain the KVG-72(*) in accordance with TB 11-7010-439-23. Complete DA Form 2404 and DA Form 2407 in accordance with DA Pam 750-8 without error. Ensure all safety precautions are observed without violation.

Special Condition: None
Special Standards: None
Special Equipment: None

Cue: Your Supervisor has directed you to troubleshoot a defective KVG-72(*).

Note: None

Performance Steps

1. Obtain required tools and test equipment.

2. Complete appropriate blocks on DA Form 2407. (DA PAM 750-8)

3. Perform visual inspection.

4. Set up/connect test equipment.

5. Verify the symptom(s), perform operational checks.

6. Proceed to PS# 12 if Unit Under Test (UUT) passes operational tests. If UUT fails, start troubleshooting PS #7.

7. Perform troubleshooting procedures.

8. Identify the fault.

9. Perform Corrective measures. If repair is not authorized proceed to step 12.

NOTE: Repair of the KVG-72 is currently limited to reloading the JOSEKI split key.

10. Verify the corrective measures corrected the fault.

11. Perform operational tests, restart at PS# 5.

12. Complete DA Form 2407. (DA PAM 750-8)

NOTE: Prepare equipment for evacuation to higher maintenance or turn in if no repair is authorized.

13. Tag defective part(s) for turn in. (DA PAM 750-8)

14. Request final inspection upon completion of task.

Evaluation Preparation:
Ensure all items required in the condition statement (or appropriate substitutions) are on hand and all safety requirements are met.

Performance Measures	GO	NO-GO
1. Obtained required tools and test equipment.	_____	_____
2. Completed appropriate blocks on DA Form 2407.	_____	_____
3. Performed visual inspection.	_____	_____
4. Set up test equipment.	_____	_____
5. Verified the symptom(s), performed operational checks.	_____	_____

	GO	NO-GO
Performance Measures		

6. Proceeded to PS# 12 if Unit Under Test (UUT) passed operational tests. If UUT failed, started troubleshooting. _____ _____

7. Performed troubleshooting procedures. _____ _____

8. Identifed the fault. _____ _____

9. Performed Corrective measures. If repair is not authorized proceeded to step 12. _____ _____

10. Verified the corrective measures corrected the fault. _____ _____

11. Performed operational tests. _____ _____

12. Completed DA Form 2407. _____ _____

13. Tagged defective part(s) for turn in. _____ _____

14. Requested final inspection. _____ _____

Evaluation Guidance: Score the soldier GO if all performance measures are passed. Score the soldier NO-GO if any performance measure is failed. If the soldier fails any performance measure, show what was done wrong and how to do it correctly.

References
Required
DA Form 2404
DA Form 2407
DA Pam 750-8
TB 11-7010-439-23
TB 385-4

Subject Area 5: Security
091-94E-1030
Implement COMSEC Security Protocol

Conditions: In an operational environment, your supervisor tasks you to Implement Communications Security (COMSEC) Protocol to identify potential incidents in a COMSEC equipment repair facility. At your disposal you have the following reference material: AR 380-40, Safeguarding And Controlling Communications Security Material; TB 380-41, Security: Procedures For Safeguarding, Accounting, and Supply Control of COMSEC Material and Local Standard Operation Procedure (SOP).

Standards: Implement COMSEC Security Protocols to Identify with 100% accuracy all potential COMSEC incidents within the repair facility. Immediately alert supervisor of all potential incidents for reporting.

Special Condition: None
Special Standards: None
Special Equipment: None

Cue: Your supervisor tasks you to Implement COMSEC Security Protocol in a COMSEC repair facility.

Note: None

Performance Steps

1. Identify potential Physical incidents.

   a. Potential incidents include but are not limited to: loss, theft, loss of control, capture, recovery by salvage, tampering, or unauthorized viewing, access or photography.

   b. Controlled Cryptographic Items (CCI), keyed or unkeyed, are included and will be reported accordingly.

2. Identify potential Cryptographic incidents.

   a. Any equipment or software malfunction, human error by an operator or COMSEC Custodian that adversely affects the cryptosecurity of a machine, auto-manual, or manual cryptosystem.

   b. Use of COMSEC keying material that is compromised, superseded, defective, or previously used (and not authorized for reuse) or incorrect application of keying material.

3. Identify potential Personnel incidents.

   a. Known or suspected absence without leave, defection, espionage, treason, or sabotage by a person having access to or a detailed knowledge of COMSEC information.

   b. Any occurrence that may jeopardize the integrity of COMSEC material or the information it protects.

29 July 2014

4. Report potential incidents to supervisor.

Evaluation Preparation:
Ensure all items required in the condition statement (or appropriate substitutions) are on hand and all safety requirements are met.

	GO	NO-GO
Performance Measures		
1. Identified potential Physical incidents.	_____	_____
2. Identified potential Cryptographic incidents.	_____	_____
3. Identified potential Personnel incidents.	_____	_____
4. Reported potential incidents to supervisor.	_____	_____

Evaluation Guidance: Score the Soldier GO if all performance measures are passed (P). Score the Soldier NO-GO if any performance measure is failed (F). If the Soldier fails any performance measure, show what was done wrong and how to do it correctly.

References
Required
AR 380-40
TB 380-41

Skill Level SL2
Subject Area 6: Maintenance Administration

091-94E-2002
Perform Tech Inspection of Radio/CCI Equipment

Conditions: In an operational environment, you are the NCO of the Radio section in an Electronic Maintenance or Shop. Your shop receives a piece of equipment with a suspected fault. You must perform a technical inspection of the equipment to classify the serviceability/reparability of the equipment prior to repair or turn-in. At your disposal you have the following items: applicable tools and technical manuals, DA Form 2404, Equipment Inspection And Maintenance Worksheet; DA Form 2407, Maintenance Request; DA Pam 750-8, The Army Maintenance Management System (TAMMS) Users Manual; TB 380-41, Security: Procedures For Safeguarding, Accounting, And Supply Control Of COMSEC Material; TB 750-90-58, Maintenance Expenditure Limits (MEL): Federal Supply Group 58, Federal; TB 43-0002-11, Maintenance Expenditure Limits, Federal Supply Groups 36, 38, 39, 45, 49 and Local Standard Operating Procedure (SOP).

Standards: Perform Technical Inspection of radio/CCI equipment in accordance with applicable technical manuals. Complete all maintenance forms and records in accordance with DA Pam 750-8, The Army Maintenance Management System (TAMMS) User Manual.

Special Condition: None
Special Standards: None
Special Equipment: None

Cue: Your shop receives a piece of radio/CCI equipment with a suspected fault. You must perform a technical inspection of the equipment to classify the serviceability/reparability of the equipment prior to repair or turn-in.

Note: None

Performance Steps

1. Obtain required tools, test equipment, and references.

2. Review operator PMCS for noted deficiencies.

3. Set up test equipment in accordance with maintenance manuals.

4. Perform technical inspection of equipment.

    a. Verify PMCS according to equipment -10.

    b. Annotate on DA FORM 2404 all faults found during the technical inspection that requires repair or replacement to restore equipment serviceability. DA PAM 750-8 Fig 3-32

    c. Determine if maintenance required is the result of fair wear and tear.

d. Determine if required maintenance/parts exceed the predetermined maintenance expenditure limit (MEL) for the equipment.

5. Complete technical inspection paperwork.

6. Complete appropriate blocks on DA Form 2407.

7. Notify supervisor upon completion of task.

Evaluation Preparation:
Ensure all items required in the condition statement (or appropriate substitutions) are on hand and all safety requirements are met.

	GO	NO-GO
Performance Measures		
1. Obtained required tools, test equipment, and references.	_____	_____
2. Reviewed operator PMCS for noted deficiencies.	_____	_____
3. Set up test equipment in accordance with maintenance manuals.	_____	_____
4. Performed technical inspection of equipment.	_____	_____
5. Completed technical inspection paperwork.	_____	_____
6. Completed appropriate blocks on DA Form 2407.	_____	_____
7. Notified supervisor upon completion of task.	_____	_____

Evaluation Guidance: Score the Soldier GO if all performance measures are passed (P). Score the Soldier NO-GO if any performance measure is failed (F). If the Soldier fails any performance measure, show what was done wrong and how to do it correctly.

References
Required
DA Form 2404
DA Form 2407
DA Pam 750-8
TB 380-41
TB 43-0002-11
TB 750-90-58

091-94E-2003
Verify Repair of Radio/CCI Equipment

Conditions: You are the section Sergeant in an Electronic Maintenance/Avionics repair facility. Your Soldiers are performing repair on a non-mission capable Radio/CCI equipment in which you must verify their progress and ensure proper procedures throughout the repair process. At your disposal you have the following: DA PAM 750-8, The Army Maintenance Management System (TAMMS) Users Manual; TB 385-4, Safety Requirements For Maintenance Of Electrical And Electronic Equipmet and Local Standard Operating Procedure (SOP).

Standards: Verify repair operations in accordance with applicable Regulations and local SOP. Ensure personnel are following all safety measures.

Special Condition: None
Special Standards: None
Special Equipment: None

Cue: You are the Section Sergeant in a Radio Repair facility.

Note: None

Performance Steps

1. Direct Soldiers on repair procedures as needed.

2. Monitor maintenance operations to ensure safety standards are being followed in accordance with unit SOPs.

3. Verify final or quality assurance/ quality control inspection of repaired equipment.

Evaluation Preparation:
Ensure all items required in the condition statement (or appropriate substitutions) are on hand and all safety requirements are met.

	GO	NO-GO
Performance Measures		
1. Advised Soldiers on repair procedures as needed.	_____	_____
2. Monitored maintenance operations to ensure safety standards were followed in accordance with unit SOPs.	_____	_____
3. Verified final or quality assurance/quality control inspection of repaired equipment.	_____	_____

Evaluation Guidance: Score the Soldier GO if all performance measures are passed (P). Score the Soldier NO-GO if any performance measure is failed (F). If the Soldier fails any performance measure, show what was done wrong and how to do it correctly.

References
Required
DA PAM 750-8

TB 385-4

091-94E-2001
React to COMSEC Insecurity

Conditions: In an operational environment, you are the Section Sergeant for a COMSEC repair facility. During the daily check you discover an event (s) that jeopardizes the security and integrity of the facility or equipment. As a precaution you report the event as a COMSEC incident. At your disposal you have the following reference material: AR 380-40, Safeguarding And Controlling Communications Security (COMSEC) Material; TB 380-41, Security: Procedures For Safeguarding, Accounting, and Supply Control of COMSEC Material and Local Standard Operation Procedure (SOP).

Standards: Identify the insecurity correctly in accordance with TB 380-41. Report the insecurity in accordance with TB 380-41.

Special Condition: None
Special Standards: None
Special Equipment: None

Cue: During the daily check of the COMSEC equipment repair facility you discover an event (s) that could jeopardize the security and integrity of the facility or equipment. As a precaution you report the incident to the proper agencies.

Note: None

Performance Steps

1. Identify the Incident.

    a. Physical Incidents.

    b. Personnel Incidents.

    c. Cryptographic Incidents.

2. Implement corrective action.

    a. Attempt to reduce or minimize the impact of the incident.

    b. Attempt to contain the incident.

3. Report insecurity.

    a. U.S. Army Counterintelligence Support Unit will be notified of all reportable COMSEC Incidents immediately upon discovery.

    b. Formal written reports are required within 24 to 72 hours depending on the type of incident.

Evaluation Preparation:
Ensure all items required in the condition statement (or appropriate substitutions) are on hand and all safety requirements are met.

	GO	NO-GO
Performance Measures		
1. Identified the incident.	_____	_____
2. Implemented corrective action.	_____	_____
3. Reported the incident to the proper agency.	_____	_____

Evaluation Guidance: Score the Soldier GO if all performance measures are passed (P). Score the Soldier NO-GO if any performance measure is failed (F). If the Soldier fails any performance measure, show what was done wrong and how to do it correctly.

References
Required
AR 380-40
TB 380-41

This page intentionally left blank.

CHAPTER 4

Duty Position Tasks

10-94E. MOS 94E--Radio and Communications Security (COMSEC) Repairer (Radio/COMSEC Rep), CMF 94

a. Major duties. The radio and COMSEC repairer performs or supervises field level maintenance on radio receivers, transmitters, COMSEC equipment, controlled cryptographic items (CCI), and associated equipment. Duties for MOS 94E at each level of skill are:

(1) MOSC 94E10. Use Test, Measurement, and Diagnostic Equipment (TMDE), Test Program Sets (TPS), and Interactive Electronic Technical Manuals (IETM) to determine the cause and location of malfunctions, extent of faults, and category of maintenance required. Inspect equipment for faults, and completeness. Test equipment to determine operational condition. Troubleshoot to determine location, and extent of equipment faults. Repair equipment by adjusting, aligning, repairing, or replacing defective components. Tests repaired equipment to ensure compliance with technical specifications. Evacuates equipment and components to higher level repair activities based on the Maintenance Allocation Chart (MAC). Prepares appropriate maintenance forms and records. Logs maintenance in accordance with The Army Maintenance Management System (TAMMS). Maintain authorized spare parts, supply stock, tool lists, technical manuals, and instructional material. Perform preventive maintenance checks and services (PMCS) on TMDE, vehicles, and power generators.

(2) MOSC 94E20. Perform duties shown in preceding skill level. Perform maintenance duties that are more complex and beyond the scope and experience of those encountered by the skill level one repairer. Provide technical assistance to both subordinates and supported users. Supervise the operation and proper use of TMDE. Schedules and performs user maintenance on TMDE, tools, and special test equipment. Perform final or quality control inspection of repaired equipment and maintenance documents. Provides shop supervisor with equipment repair status, priorities, and necessity for bench stock resupply. Maintain maintenance facility technical library. Ensures that National Security Agency (NSA) approved components are used in COMSEC/CCI repairs. Controls and accounts for COMSEC/CCI within the repair facility.

(3) MOSC 94E30. Perform duties shown in preceding skill level. Performs maintenance duties that are more complex and beyond the scope and experience of those encountered by the skill level two repairer. Supervises and leads sections or squads of electronic repairers. Establishes workload, work schedules, and repair priorities. Assign priority of work for job requests. Supervise final or quality control inspection of repaired equipment and maintenance documents. Supervise calibration and shop safety programs. Ensures repair functions comply with Army and NSA COMSEC/CCI specifications and policies.

b. Physical demands rating and qualifications for initial award of MOS. Radio and COMSEC repairer must possess the following qualifications:
    (1) A physical demands rating of heavy.
    (2) A physical profile of 111221.
    (3) Qualifying Scores.

    (a) A minimum score of 105 in aptitude area EL on Armed Services Vocational Aptitude Battery (ASVAB) tests administered prior to 2 January 2002.

    (b) A minimum score of 102 in aptitude area EL on ASVAB tests administered on and after 2 January 2002.

    (4) A security eligibility of SECRET.

    (5) A U.S citizen.

    (6) Formal training by completion of the MOS 94E Course conducted under the auspices of the U.S. Army Ordnance School (USAOS) is mandatory unless a waiver is granted by Commandant, U.S. Army Ordnance School (USAOS), Fort Lee, VA 23801.

    (7) Must be certified as COMSEC equipment repairer contained in AR 25-12.

    c. Additional skill identifiers. (Note: Refer to table 12-8 (Listing of universal ASI's associated with all enlisted MOS)).

    (1) Y2--Transition (Personnel only).

    (2) Y3—-Transition (Personnel only).

    d. Physical requirements and standards of grade. Physical requirements and SG relating to each skill level are listed in the following tables:

    (1) Table 10-94E-1. Physical requirements.

    (2) Table 10-94E-2. Standards of grade TOE/MTOE.

    (3) Table 10-94E-3. Standards of grade TDA.

Table 10-94E-1
Physical requirements for MOS 94E

Skill Level	Task numbers	Tasks
1	1,2,3,4	1. Occasionally lifts 175 pounds 4 feet as part of a 2 soldier team (prorated 88 pounds per soldier) and carries 25 feet (can be carried intermittently)..
2	1,2,3,4	2. Occasionally lifts/lowers 75 pounds 4 feet and carries 25 feet (can be carried intermittently. Must possess normal color vision
3	1,2,3,4	3. Must possess normal color vision.
		4. . Must possess finger dexterity in both hands.

Table 10-94E-2
Standards of Grade TOE/MTOE

Line	Duty Position	Code	Grade	Number of Positions										Explanatory notes
				1	2	3	4	5	6	7	8	9	10	
1	COMSEC/Radio Equip RPR	94E10	E3		1	1	2	2	2					1. Grades of additional positions will be in same pattern and applied cumulatively to all positions at section level. 2. Grading pattern will be used for all positions not specifically identified in any other line.
2	COMSEC/Radio Equip RPR	94E10	E4	1	1	1	1	2	2					
3	SR COMSEC/RADIO RPR	94E20	E5			1	1	1	1					
4	COMSEC/RADIO SUPV	94E30	E6						1					
5	COMSEC/Radio Equip RPR	94E10 94E1S	E4	1	1	1	2	3	4	5				1. Strategic Signal Det. 2. TAC Inst/Network Co Teams. 3. Two person COMSEC Maint Teams. 4. RPV Equip Repair Teams. 5. Hg, SOA Regt. 6. GP Svc Spt Co, SF GP Spt Bn, Elect Maint Sec (31828Gxxx)
6	SR SOMSEC/RADIO RPR	94E20	E5		1	1	1	1	1	1				
7	COMSEC/RADIO SUPV	94E30	E6			1	1	1	1	1				1. CINC Commo Teams. 2. Joint Task Force. As single MOS 94E position in: a. Sig Co, Bde Cbt Tm. b. COMMEL Team. c. Wpn Sys Rcvry Team.
8	SR COMSEC/RADIO RPR	94E30	E6	1	1	2	2	3	4	5	6			
9	COMSEC/RADIO SUPV	94E30	E6		1	1	2	2	2	2	2			
10	SR COMSEC/RADIO RPR	94E20	E5											
11	RADIO REP QA/QC TI	94E20	E5											Principal MOS 94E Quality Control NCO in organization performing maint on COMSEC/Radio equipment.
12	COMSEC/RADIO SUPV	94E30	E6											1. Armed Forces Info Spt Tm. 2. TAC Inst/Network Co. 3. Hq, Spt Bn, Hvy Sep Bde. 4. MMC, Corps Spt Cmd. 5. MMC, TA. 6. MMC, Theater Spt Cmd.
13	PLATOON SERGEANT	94E30	E6											Principal NCO in a platoon with platoon leader and nine or fewer enlisted subordinates

Notes:
1. *Blank spaces in this column indicate not applicable.
2. Unless otherwise noted in explanatory notes, single lines provide grading for one position only.
3. When TOE/MTOE organizations are supported by an augmentation TDA, augmentation (A) and base paragraphs will be graded in the aggregate.
4. When no grading guidance is provided by this table for coding TOE/MTOE, TRADOC MSCs and Non-TRADOC specified proponent (TOE Combat Developers) will coordinate with appropriate Branch Personnel Proponents (listed in chapter 15) to support additional grading of manpower requirements.

Table 10-94E-3
Standards of Grade TDA

Line	Duty Position	Code	Grade	1	2	3	4	5	6	7	8	9	10	Explanatory notes
				\multicolumn{10}{Number of Positions}										
1	COMSEC/Radio Equip RPR	94E10	E3			1	2	2	2	2	2	2	2	1. Grades of additional
2	COMSEC/Radio Equip RPR	94E10	E4		1	1	1	2	2	3	4	5	5	positions will be in same
3	SR COMSEC/RADIO RPR	94E20	E5	1	1	1	1	1	1	1	1	1	1	pattern and applied
4	COMSEC/RADIO SUPV	94E30	E6							1	1		1	2	cumulatively to all positions at section level. 2. Grading pattern will be used for all positions not specifically identified in any other line.
5	COMSEC/Radio Equip RPR	94E10 94E1S	E4	1	1	2	3	3	4					Comm MGT Spt Tm (CMST) in 1108th Sig Bde.
6	SR SOMSEC/RADIO RPR	94E20	E5		1	1	1	2	2					
7	COMSEC/RADIO SUPV	94E30	E6											1. Numbers in (#) indicate total of multiple positions in organization. 2. 1111th Sig, Ft Ritche (10).
8	SR COMSEC/RADIO RPR	94E30	E6											1. Numbers in (#) indicate total of multiple positions in organization. 2. USAE Allied Cmd Eur (ACE) (10). 3. USAE Allied Forces South (AFSOUTH) (5). 4. USAE Allied Forces South East Europe (ALFSEE) (8). 5. 1111th Sig, Ft Ritche (16). 6. DoD Agencies (4). 7. Hq, 59th Ord.
9	COMSEC/RADIO SUPV	94E30	E6											1. Numbers in (#) indicate total of multiple positions in organization. 2. USAE White House Comm Agcy (WHCA) (46). 3. USAE ACE (9). 4. USAE AFSOUTH (7). 5. USAE ALFSEE (12). 6. 1111th Sig, Ft Ritche (3). 7. Hq, U.S. Forces Korea (2). 8. DoD Agencies. 9. U.S. E4 Ops Cmd (2). 10. USAE Joint Cmd Spt Elm, McDill AFB (6).

	Duty Position	Code	Grade	Number of Positions										Explanatory notes
				1	2	3	4	5	6	7	8	9	10	
10	COMSEC RADIO SUPV	94E30	E6			3								1. Numbers in (#) indicate total of multiple positions in organization. 2. USAE WHCA (12). 3. USAE ACE (3). 4. USAE AFSOUTH (4). 5. USAE ALFSEE (4). 6. 1111th Sig, Ft Ritche (3). 7. Hq, U.S. Forces Korea. 8. Hq, STARC (ARNG) (2). 9. USAG Ft Wainwright. 10. DoD Agencies (2). 11. U.S. E4 Ops Cmd. 12. Hq, INSCOM (2). 13. AMC Europe (3). 14. 1110the Sig Bn. 15. Army Ops Ctr. 16. USAE DISA Europe. 17. Hq, DISA JITC. 18. USA MAINT ACT, Europe. 19. A Btry, 1st Bn, Ft Sill. 20. U.S. Army Tng/Sec Cmd, Kuwait. 21. USAE IBERLANT, Lisbon. 22. Hq, U.S. Army SWA. 23. USA Sig Act, Ft Gordon. 24. USA Sig Act, Arl Hall. 25. USA INSCOM Mission, Ft Belvoir (2). 26. USAR USAG. Subsequent positions also graded E6.
11	COMSEC/Radio Equip RPR	94E10	E6											Principal NCO in a platoon with platoon leader and nine or fewer enlisted subordinates.

Notes:
1. *Blank spaces in this column indicate not applicable.
2. Unless otherwise noted in explanatory notes, single lines provide grading for one position only.
3. When TDA organizations are supported with additional and/or dual line TDA positions, the additional line(s) and base paragraph will be graded in the aggregate.
4. When no grading guidance is provided by this table for coding TDA, ACOM Manpower Managers will coordinate with the appropriate Branch Personnel Proponents (listed inchapter 15) to support additional grading of manpower requirements.

This page intentionally left blank.

GLOSSARY

Section I
Acronyms & Abbreviations

AN/PRC	Army Navy / Personnel Radio Communication
DA FORM	Department of the Army Form
DA PAM	Department of the Army pamphlet
MX	Mechanized
NSN	National Stock Number
PM	Preventive Maintenance
RT	Receiver Transmitter
SINAD (1)	Signal-plus-noise-plus-distortion to noise-plus-distortion ratio.
SOP	Standing Operating Procedure
TB	Technical bulletin
TM	Technical manual
TS	Top Secret

Section II
Terms

National Stock Number
The 13-digit stock number replacing the 11-digit Federal Stock Number. It consists of the 4-digit Federal Supply Classification code and the 9-digit National Item Identification Number. The National Item Identification Number consists of a 2-digit National Codification Bureau number designating the central cataloging office (whether North Atlantic Treaty Organization or other friendly country) that assigned the number and a 7-digit (xxx-xxxx) nonsignificant number. The number shall be arranged as follows: 9999-00-999-9999. Also called NSN.

Technical manual (TM)
A publication that describes equipment, weapons, or weapons systems with instructions for effective use. It may include sections for instructions covering initial preparation for use and operational maintenance and overhaul.

This page intentionally left blank.

REFERENCES

Required Publications
Required publications are sources that users must read in order to understand or to comply with
this publication. Most Army doctrinal publications are available online: www.apd.army.mil.

ADRP 1-02. Terms and Military Symbols. 24 September 2014.
AR 380-40. Safeguarding and Controlling Communications Security Material. 9 July 2012.
DA PAM 750-8. The Army Maintenance Management System (TAMMS) Users Manual. 22 August 2005.
FM 21-11. First Aid for Soldiers. 27 October 1988.

Most joint publications are available online: www.dtic.mil/doctrine/new_pubs/jointpub.htm.

JP 1-02. Department of Defense Dictionary of Military and Associated Symbols. 8 November 2010.
TB 11-5820-1130-30. Warranty Program for Radio Set, AN/PSC-5. 1 March 2002.
TB 11-7010-439-23. Field Testing and Assembly Instructions for Force XXI Battle Command Brigade and Below (FBCB2) Fault Verification Test Kit (KVTK). 15 June 2008.
TB 43-0002-11. Maintenance Expenditure Limits, Federal Supply Groups 36, 38, 39, 45, 49, 54, 58, 61, 66, 67, 69, 74, 81; Federal Supply Classes 5805, 5815, 5820, 5821, 5825, 5826, 5830, 5831, 5835, 5840, 5841, 5845, 5850, 5855, 5860, 5865, 5895, 5905, 5910, 5915, 5920, 5925, 5930, 5935, 5940, 5945, 5950, 5955, 5960, 5961, 5962, 5965, 5970, 5975, 5977, 5985, 5990, 5995, 5999, 6125, 6130, 6135, 6140, 6145, 6615, 6625, 6660, 6695, 6710, 6720, 6730, 6740, 6750, 6760, 6770, 6780, 6940, 7450, 8130. 2 May 1997.
TB 380-41. Security: Procedures for Safeguarding, Accounting and Supply Control of Comsec Material. 08/15/2013.
TB 385-4. Safety Requirements for Maintenance of Electrical and Electronic Equipment. 1 July 2008.
TB 750-90-58. Maintenance Expenditure Limits (MEL): Federal Supply Group 58, Federal Supply Class 5810. 6 December 1991.
TM 1-1680-377-13&P-2. Technical Manual Operator's, Unit, and Direct Support Maintenance Manual Including Repair Parts and Special Tools List for Radio Set AN/PRC-90 NSN 5820-00-782-5308 Radio Set AN/PRC-90-2 NSN 5820-01-238-6603 RADIO SET AN/PRC-112 NSN 5820-01-279-5450 Program Loader KY-913/PRC-112 NSN 7025-01-279-5308. 23 March 2012.
TM 11-5810-394-13&P. Operator and Field Maintenance Manual (Including Repair Parts and Special Tools List (RPSTL)) FOR AN/CYZ-10 V3 (NSN 5810-01-393-1973) Data Transfer Device Using CT3 (V3.2) User Application Software and NSA FILL 5.7 User Application Software. 06/20/2007.
TM 11-5810-410-13&P. Operators and Field Maintenance Manual Including Repair Parts and Special Tools List for Transfer Unit, Cryptographic Key AN/PYQ-10(C) Simple Key Loader (SKL) SKL UAS Version 7.2 (NSN 5810-01-517-3587). 15 August 2013.

TM 11-5820-890-30. Intermediate (Direct Support) Maintenance Manual Receiver-Transmitter, Radio RT-1439/VRC (NSN 5820-01-195-0827); Amplifier-Adapter, Vehicular AM-7239/VRC (5895-01-188-8819); Amplifier, Radio Frequency AM-7238/VRC (5895-01-195-4844); Control-Monitor C-11291/VRC (5820-01-151-9914); Mounting Base, Electrical Equipment MT-6352/VRC (5975-01-188-8873); Battery Box CY-8346/PRC (6135-01-188-8859); Mounting Base, Electrical Equipment MT-6353/VRC (5975-01-235-1962); Maintenance Group OA-9263/GRC (6625-01-230-2352); Mounting Base, Electrical Equipment MT-6429/VRC (5820-01-220-7901). 1 March 1988.

TM 11-5820-890-30P-1. Direct Support Maintenance Repair Parts and Special Tools List for Radio Sets AN/PRC-119 (NSN 5820-01-151-9915) AN/PRC-119A (5820-01-267-9482) AN/PRC-119D (5820-01-421-0801) AN/VRC-87 (5820-01-151-9916) AN/VRC-87A (5820-01-267-9480) AN/VRC-87D (5820-01-351-5259) (EIC: GAR) AN/VRC-88 (5820-01-151-9917) AN/VRC-88A (5820-01-267-9481) AN/VRC-88D (5820-01-352-1694) AN/VRC-89 (5820-01-151-9918) (EIC: L2V) AN/VRC-89A (5820-01-267-9479) AN/VRC-89D (5820-01-420-6619) AN/VRC-90 (5820-01-151-9919) AN/VRC-90A (5820-01-268-5105) AN/VRC-90D (5820-01-420-6618) (EIC: GD9) AN/VRC-91 (5820-01-151-9920) AN/VRC-91A (5820-01-267-9478) AN/VRC-91D (5820-01-420-6621) AN/VRC-92 (5820-01-151-9921) (EIC: L2Y) AN/VRC-92A (5820-01-267-9477) AND AN/VRC-92D (5820-01-421-2605). 30 November 2002.

TM 11-5820-890-30P-2. Direct Support Maintenance Repair Parts and Special Tools List for Receiver-Transmitter, Radio RT-1523A(C)/U,RT-1523D(C)/U (5820-01-410-8981) Mounting Base, Electrical Equipment MT-6352A/VRC (5975-01-304-2050) Control-Monitor C-11291A/VRC (5895-01-309-1309) Battery Box CY-8523B/PRC (6160-01-304-2034) Amplifier, Radio Frequency AM-7238A/VRC (5895-01-306-8093) Amplifier-Adapter, Vehicular AM-7239A/VRC (5895-01-304-8389) Amplifier-Adapter, Vehicular AM-7239D/VRC (5895-01-422-8781). 1 September 1998.

TM 11-5820-890-30P-3. Direct Support and Maintenance Repair Parts and Special Tools List for Radio Sets AN/PRC-119F (NSN 5820-01-451-8252) AN/VRC-87F (5820-01-451-8248) AN/VRC-88F (5820-01-452-8435) AN/VRC-89F (5820-01-451-8247) AN/VRC-90F (5820-01-451-8246) AN/VRC-91F (5820-01-451-8249) (EIC: N/A) AND AN/VRC-92F (5820-01-451-8250). 30 November 2002.

TM 11-5820-1037-13&P. Operator's, Unit, And Intermediate Maintenance Manual (Repair Parts And Special Tools List) For Radio Set AN/PRC-112 (NSN 5820-01-279-5450) Program Loader KY-913/PRC-112 (NSN 7025-01-279-5308). 15 July 2005.

TM 11-5820-1049-12. Operator's and Aviation Unit Maintenance Manual for Radio Set AN/PRC-90-2 (NSN 5820-01-238-6603). 15 August 1990.

TM 11-5820-1049-30. Aviation Intermediate Maintenance Manual for Radio Set AN/PRC-90-2 (NSN 5820-01-238-6603). 15 August 1990.

TM 11-5820-1130-30&P. Direct Support Maintenance Manual (Including Repair Parts and Special Tools List) for Radio Set AN/PSC-5 (NSN 5820-01-366-4120) {TO 31R2-2PSC5-2; NAVELEX EE125-WU-MMO-010/PSC-5; TM 10191A-30&P/2}. 15 March 1997.

TM 11-5821-318-30P. Aviation Unit Maintenance Repair Parts and Special Tools List for VHF AM/FM RADIO SET AN/ARC-186(V) (NSN 5821-01-086-6243) (EIC: N/A). 1 September 2005.

TM 11-5821-333-13&P-1. Operator and Field Maintenance Manual Including Repair Parts and Special Tools List for Sincgars Airborne Icom and Non-Icom Combat Net Radios Non-Icom Airborne Radio AN/ARC-201(V) , ICOM Airborne Radio AN/ARC-201A(V), PI ICOM Airborne Radio AN/ARC-201C(V), SIP ICOM Airborne Radio AN/ARC-201D(V). 15May 2013.

TM 11-5821-333-13&P-2. Operator and Field Maintenance Manual Including Repair Parts and Special Tools List for Sincgars Airborne ICOM and NON-ICOM Combat Net Radios Non-Icom Airborne Radio AN/ARC-201(V) , ICOM Airborne Radio AN/ARC-201A(V), PI ICOM Airborne Radio AN/ARC-201C(V), SIP ICOM Airborne Radio AN/ARC-201D(V). 15 May 2013.

TM 11-5821-356-23. Aviation Unit and Intermediate Maintenance Manual for Radio Set AN/ARC-164 Radio Receiver-Transmitters RT-1145F, RT-1167, RT-1167A, RT-1167B, RT-1167C, RT-1167G, RT-1167H, RT-1504, RT-1518, RT-1518A, RT-1518B, RT-1518C, AND RT-1614 Radio Set Controls C-9682B AND C-11721 Electrical Equipment Mounting Bases MT-4708 AND MT-4838. 1 March 1996.

TM 11-5895-1174-23. Aviation Unit and Intermediate Maintenance Manual for Control, Aviation Unit Communication System C-6533/ARC (NSN: 5895-00-895-4175) and C-6533A/ARC (5895-01-491-9407) Aviation Unit Maintenance. 15 November 2005.

TM 11-5895-1174-23P. Aviation Unit and Intermediate Maintenance Repair Parts and Special Tools List for Control, Communications System C-6533/ARC (NSN 5831-00-895-4175) AND C-6533A/ARC (5895-01-491-9407). 1 April 1991.

TM 11-6130-233-12. Operators and Organizational Maintenance Manual: Power Supplies, PP-2953/U, PP-2953A/U, PP-2953B/U AND PP-2953C/U (NSN 6130-00-985-7899). 9 January 1984.

TM 11-6130-233-24P. Organizational, Direct Support, and General Support Maintenance Repair Parts and Special Tools List for Power Supply: PP-2953/U, PP-2953A/U, PP-2953B/U, AND PP-2953C/U (NSN 6130-00-985-7899). 15 December 1988.

TM 11-6130-233-35. Direct Support, General Support, and Depot Maintenance Manual for Power Supplies, PP-2953/U, PP-2953A/U, PP-2953B/U AND PP-2953C/U (NSN 6130-00-985-7899). 18 March 1965.

TM 11-6130-266-15. Operator`s, Organizational, Direct Support, General Support, and Depot Maintenance Manual (Including Repair Parts and Special Tools List) for Power Supply, PP-6224/U AND PP-6224A/U (NSN 6130-00-133-5879) (Reprinted W/BASIC INCL C1-4). 23 September 1971.

TM 11-6130-266-24P-2. Organizational, Direct Support, and General Support Maintenance Repair Parts and Special Tools Lists for Power Supply PP-6224A/U (NSN 6130-00-133-5879). 31 July 1978.

TM 11-6625-3300-10. Technical Manual Operator`s Manual for Plug-in Unit, Electronic Test Equipment PL-1536/GRM (NSN 6625-01-432-3819) Plug-in Unit, Electronic Test Equipment PL-1549/GRM (NSN 6625-01-565-7494) Plug-in Unit, Electronic Test Equipment PL-1550/GRM (NSN 6625-01-558-6903) Plug-In Unit, Electronic Test Equipment PL-1553/GRM (NSN 6625-01-570-5868) and Power Supply PP-8571/GRM (NSN 6130-01-573-0829) When Used with Radio Test Set AN/GRM-122 (NSN 6625-01-309-2825). 30 March 2011.

Related Publications

Related publications are sources of additional information. They are not required in order to understand this publication.

ADRP 7-0. Training Units and Developing Leaders, 23 August 2012.

Recommended Readings

TM 11-6625-928-35. Direct Support, General Support, and Depot Maintenance Manual for Test Facilities Kit, MK-994/AR (NSN 6625-00-802-7191) AND MK-994A/AR (6625-01-189-7882). 9 December 1968.

TM 11-6625-3016-10-1. Operators Manual for Radio Test Set, AN/GRM-114A (NSN 6625-01-144-4481). 20 June 1983.

Prescribed Forms

None.

Referenced Forms

Unless otherwise indicated, DA forms are available on the Army Publishing Directorate (APD) Web site: www.apd.army.mil.

DA Form 2028. Recommended Changes to Publications and Blank Forms.
DA Form 2404. Equipment Inspection and Maintenance Worksheet.
DA Form 2407. Maintenance Request.

By order of the Secretary of the Army:

RAYMOND T. ODIERNO
General, United States Army
Chief of Staff

Official:

GERALD B. O'KEEFE
Administrative Assistant to the
Secretary of the Army
1419601

DISTRIBUTION:

Active Army, Army National Guard, and United States Army Reserve: Distributed in electronic media only (EMO).

PIN: 104465-000

www.ingramcontent.com/pod-product-compliance
Lightning Source LLC
Chambersburg PA
CBHW080338290526
45790CB00010B/3754